ATLANTIC EDITIONS draw from *The Atlantic*'s rich literary history and robust coverage of the driving cultural and political forces of today. Each book features long-form journalism by *Atlantic* writers devoted to a single topic, focusing on contemporary articles or classic storytelling from the magazine's 165-year archive.

ON
THINKING FOR YOURSELF

Instinct, Education, Dissension

CAITLIN FLANAGAN

zando
NEW YORK

For Jeffrey Goldberg,
a friend when I really needed one

CONTENTS

INTRODUCTION

IF YOU'VE TAKEN A college tour lately, either as an applicant or the parent of an applicant, you will notice that at some point—usually as you're on the death march from the aquatic center to the natural sciences complex—the tour guide will spin smartly on her heel, do the college tour guide thing of performatively walking backward, and let you in on something very important. "What's different about College X," she'll say confidently, "is that our professors don't teach you *what* to think. They teach you *how* to think."

Whether or not you've heard the phrase before, it gets your attention. Can anyone teach you how to think? Aren't we all thinking all the time, isn't the proof of our existence found in our think, think, thinking, one banal thought at a time?

The tour eventually ends, and in a couple of hours you're on another college campus, and while you're marching from that institution's climbing gym to its sophomore student housing, a different tour guide spins on his heel, speeds up, and lets you in on his school's secret: "What's different about College Y," he says—with what seems to be complete confidence that you haven't heard such a thing before—"is that our professors don't teach us what to think; they teach us *how* to think."

Each of the guides seems to think this is a point of difference about his or her college, which is itself a sign that they have spent a lot more time in the "what to think" school of higher education than in the "how to think" one. When you're visiting a college, walk through the corridors of some of the humanities departments. Look at the posters advertising upcoming events and speakers, read the course listings, or just stand silent in front of the semiotic overload of the instructors' office doors, where wild declarations of what they think and what they plan to make you think will be valorously displayed.

Does this look like a department that is going to teach you how to think?

TO THE EXTENT THAT I have learned to think for myself, it's because my father taught me how to do it. Usually by asking me a single question.

For the love of God, I hated that question. And for some reason I always, always forgot to see it coming. My father was an academic and a writer and he cared a great deal about teaching, and he was never off the clock.

There we'd be, chatting away when some new subject or other would heave into view, and I'd launch into a long assessment of it. I'd be certain—absolutely positive—that

I was right. My father would listen, head cocked a little to the side, often smiling a bit, sometimes raising his eyebrows after an especially bold point. For some reason I would feel encouraged—not wary—and I'd bash ahead into bolder assessments.

Eventually, I'd run out of steam and finish up, with some sort of gesture meaning "case closed."

There would be a moment of silence. And then my father would say—gently, because there was zero need to say it any other way: "And what is the best argument of the other side?"

The best argument of the other side! Jesus Christ—*the other side?* The whole point of the argument was to destroy the other side! I was there to illuminate and then devastate the other side by engaging deeply with the worst it had to offer.

Which is usually a light lift.

I had learned the style and the rhetorical turns of making a great case, but I didn't know the first thing about fortifying it with facts, reason, logic—or the best argument of the side I was treating in such a cavalier way.

You don't have to delve into the arcana of the Third Reich to destroy anyone making a case for it. But these layups rarely present themselves in decent places. Most of the time the subjects we talk about are—for all of their flattening by cable news and internet wormholes and all the rest of it—extremely complicated.

A teacher should never do your thinking for you. She should give you texts to read and guide you along the path of making sense of them for yourself. She should introduce you to the books and essays of writers who disagree with one another and ask you to determine whose case is better.

Many college professors don't want to do that today. They don't want to "platform" a writer they think is wrong; they don't want to participate in "both side-ism." The same thing is true for the students who pound on the doors of lecture halls and pull fire alarms and throw garbage cans down hallways to protest the 45-minute speech of a visitor.

That professor and those college students believe in sympathetic magic. They believe that words—even those spoken within a lecture hall they can't get into—will damage them and their classmates. The truth is that they're scared. They don't think their ideas can outmatch those of the hated speaker.

Is there anything more satisfying than watching a debate in which the sophist gets defenestrated by someone smarter, better prepared, and obviously right?

Don't bang on the doors of the lecture hall. Book this character in the biggest auditorium you have. Broadcast him live on a campus radio station. Tell him the only requirement for his visit is that he engage in debate with one of your students—and then track down the young

A

woman or man who owns this subject. And the professors who can help him or her to make the strongest possible case.

Do you think evil can stand up against that student's case? It can't.

The truth bats last.

This little book is a collection of essays I wrote for *The Atlantic* that emanates from my stubborn desire to think for myself. Any time a person in authority tells me that I must believe their version of events—even when the truth is so obviously different—has my attention. Some of them are about very serious subjects, such as the brutal attack on Salman Rushdie or the media's certainty that a video of an adolescent on the Washington Mall shows him committing a hate crime. Others are about extremely nonserious subjects, such as . . . well, you'll see. They all come from the same impulse, however—and they are certainly a product of George Orwell's observation that "to see what is in front of one's nose needs a constant struggle."

It's more true now than in his day: Here is what you have to believe to be a "good" person—someone "clubbable," to use an old phrase—and here are the facts on the ground.

I can tell you that each time I finished one of these essays, I heard a tiny, satisfying kind of "click." I had done the best I could to find out what had happened, correct the record, and draw a conclusion supported by facts.

The world is full of glittering images and salesmen eager to get you to buy one of them. But it's your life and your mind, and—as of present writing—you have every right to think and speak and write for yourself. You're needed out here.

One last thing—that phrase the confident tour guides are throwing at you about this or that college being the place to teach you how vs. what to think? They'd cut it out of the spiel if they knew who came up with it.

Socrates.

"I can't teach anybody anything. All I can do is make them think."

CAITLIN FLANAGAN

April 2023

A

CAROLINE CALLOWAY
ISN'T A SCAMMER

September 2019

LET US BEGIN WITH THE 45 SERVINGS of eggplant salad made in the tiny kitchen of a studio apartment in Greenwich Village, transported to a Brooklyn loft, and served as a homemade lunch to ticketed guests. It was so tasty that many people asked for—and were generously given, at no extra cost—second helpings. And let us acknowledge that if this labor-intensive, potentially money-losing endeavor were part of a "scam"—as many people insist that it was—its architect may not be suited to the life. If you are running a short con that involves driving eggplant salad to another borough, you might as well find honest work, because you lack the grifter mentality.

Now let's back up.

Caroline Calloway came crashing into my awareness, and maybe into yours, this month when a former friend of hers, Natalie Beach, published a revenge essay in *The Cut* titled "I Was Caroline Calloway." It was a sensation, as there are only two possible positions vis-à-vis this young woman: You've never heard of her, or you possess a nearly encyclopedic amount of information about her. She is an Instagram "influencer" with close to 800,000 followers, and it seemed as though within 24 hours every single one of them had blazed through the piece and made some kind of comment about it on social media. The majority of her followers are young white women, a demographic not underrepresented in the world of media, and so—improbably enough—this micro-event was covered just about everywhere, including in the *New York Times*, the *Washington Post*, NBC, you name it.

Natalie chose her moment wisely and kicked Caroline when she was down: First, Caroline had sold a book proposal for a large sum of money, then failed to deliver the manuscript and had to pay back the portion of the advance she'd been given. In January, she'd had the idea to host a series of "creativity workshops" for her fans, offering to spend time with them; giving them gifts, some of them handmade; and serving lunch—including that eggplant salad. But the organizational skills required to manage these events overwhelmed her. She ended up canceling most of the workshops, and the ticketing agency Eventbrite refunded everyone. For this, she has become known as an internet scammer, on a par with the men who organized the notorious Fyre Festival. Any time investors or ticket holders are given a prompt, full refund, you are not anywhere near the land of the scam, but the internet didn't care.

All influencers live on the knife's edge. To display the details of an appealing life is to gather fans and jealous toads at about a 5-to-1 ratio. Get big enough, and then make a mistake, and the toads will rise up. Female internet rage is not nearly as frightening as male internet rage, which can include threats of extreme violence and sexual harm. But what it lacks in physical threats, it can make up for in intensity. Once it is unleashed on a new victim, all she can really do is lie low and wait it out; although, this is not the way of an Instagrammer, who inevitably prolongs the attack by repeatedly posting about it.

The venom of Natalie's essay in no way matches her claims against Caroline, which amount to these: For a short period, Natalie helped edit Caroline's posts, a service for which she was compensated, and she ghostwrote the book proposal, for which she requested the astronomical fee of 35 percent. For the toads, this news of a ghostwriter was the last straw. Caroline's creativity workshops had been a scam, and now it seemed that she herself was a fraud.

Grotesquely, two days after the publication of the story in *The Cut*, the bloated body of Caroline's mentally ill father was discovered in his home, a possible suicide. He may have been dead for more than a week. Some of the toads announced, in what they seemed to think was a high-minded stance, that they would not discuss the death. Others felt no need to hold back. On the day

Caroline announced her father's death, someone commented on her heartfelt post: "Just fucking deleted your social media. Nobody gives a shit about your [sic]." I started to worry. With a gathering sense of unease, it occurred to me that these bitches might actually kill her.

Caroline Gotschall was born in the middle-class but by no means glamorous suburb of Falls Church, Virginia. "It wasn't one of those REALLY bougie suburbs," she tells us, "where the politicians live, with the sweeping lawns and the azaleas." Rather, it was more "parking lots and Best Buys and craft stores." Falls Church is one of those American towns determined to think of itself, in terms both gently self-mocking and obviously self-congratulatory, as a *Mayberry R.F.D.* kind of place. In Falls Church, the ethos of swim teams and Little League games and Reunion Sundays prevails, and despite profound changes in the racial demographics of the Washington, DC, metro area, it remains overwhelmingly white. Caroline was the only child of an unhappy mother and a mentally ill father. (Unless otherwise noted, all information about Caroline comes from her Instagram account. I don't know if it is all the truth, but as we say today, it is "her truth," and I read it as such.)

When Caroline was 7, her parents separated. Her mother moved herself and her daughter out of the family house, a place that quickly became a monument to her father's illness, a site of hoarding and disrepair. It was in this house that his body was discovered. He had a terrible temper, which was surely frightening to the little girl who, in the way of all daughters, wanted only approval, protection, and love from the most powerful man in her life. She understood him to be profoundly intelligent—"a rain man savant"—and clearly his belief in the value of education pursued at the most elite and storied institutions was a preoccupation he impressed upon his daughter. He insisted that Caroline attend a fancy private school in Alexandria, 45 minutes away from Falls Church. Caroline's mother objected, but she was worn down by him, and thus began a ritual, born of necessity, of the father driving the little girl to and from school. That so much of their private time unfolded in the course of pursuing an elite education is entirely fitting. It is the force that allied them most powerfully.

Once, Caroline asked her father what had been the happiest day of his life. It took him a long time to think of an answer, presumably not because there had been so many of them, but rather because the taxonomic consideration of "happiest days" was not one he dwelled on very often. Finally, he came up with the perfect answer: the day she was born. Of all of the things I have learned about this tragic man through his daughter's various accounts of him, this was the most poignant. When an only child asks you about the happiest day of your life, there is only one right one, and he had found it.

Secure in her father's affections, Caroline told him she wanted to hear a story that didn't involve her, and he told her that the second-happiest day of his life had been the day he was admitted to Harvard. He'd sat on his bed with the course catalog, marveling at all the classes in all the many departments, the whole world revealed to him in this book of offerings. But her father did not simply love Harvard for the education it could offer him. He loved it for all the old reasons: its history and traditions and rituals. He told her that he had been "number two" at the *Crimson*, filling her mind with lore about the rivalry between the *Crimson* and the *Lampoon*. He had gone to Harvard from Exeter, a double cynosure. Only when she was a young woman did she learn from one of his boarding-school classmates that he'd been somewhat of a laughing-stock there, nicknamed "Briefcase Bill" for the uncool way he carried his books and notes to class in an attaché case. Preppies can be their own kind of toad.

As a child, Caroline was sad and desperately lonely. She was bullied at school, upset about the divorce, and trying her best to contend with her father's mental illness and depression. She became the kind of girl who rebelled against these things not by getting in trouble, but by building an imaginary world for herself and then moving into it. She filled her bedroom with art supplies and books about princesses and fairies and magic. She had a Union Jack on the wall, and she went through a *Titanic* phase.

She loved *Harry Potter*, and she kept a framed photograph of her very favorite aristocrat, Empress Sisi of Austria, who was known for her great beauty, her slender figure, and her luxuriant long hair, into which she sometimes braided flowers. Caroline stared out her bedroom windows—which gave way only to a boring suburban street in boring Falls Church—and thought about her future. She spent all her time "waiting, waiting, waiting" for her life to begin.

She applied to Exeter, but she was rejected. It's a delicate thing for the child of an alumnus to get rejected from the parent's school. What most parents do is move on very quickly and settle the child in a different school, but Caroline says she was rejected over and over by the institution. That's a punishing process, and one born of obsession. Whose was the obsession—Caroline's, or her father's? Or was it a shared obsession, one Caroline adopted to draw closer to her father? And how does a teenager ever gain a sense of real belonging at an elite institution—Exeter is widely regarded as the most prestigious boarding school in the country—if it has rejected her so many times? If you have to push harder and harder on the golden door until it is grudgingly wedged open just wide enough and long enough for you to dart through it, have you sullied the project? Finally, the door swung open just wide enough for her to dart in for her senior year. At age 17, she changed her name to Caroline Calloway—it sounded more like that of a writer, she has said. Maybe it also sounded more like that of someone who would have been admitted to Exeter the first time around.

Her college-admissions process, as she describes it, was similar to the failure-is-not-an-option war she waged on Exeter. She applied to Yale, Harvard, Oxford, and Cambridge not once, but apparently four times over four years. Finally, St Edmund's College—which she had strategically chosen, she says, because it was the least desired of the Oxbridge colleges and therefore gave her the best odds—waved the white flag and admitted her, a 22-year-old "first year student." Life could begin.

Caroline characterizes the three years between boarding school and Cambridge as a series of gap years, which is straining the term of art to the breaking point, and also a flagrant denial of something that happened IRL: enrolling at NYU, which most people would consider putting an end to the gap years and starting college. Not Caroline. It was just one of those things that happened while you were staring out the bedroom window, waiting. But we must not pass over these years, because this is where she met her future, poisonous diarist, when both enrolled in a creative-nonfiction class. Let that be a lesson on creative-nonfiction classes.

And let us now admit Natalie's essay to our list of sources. Here she is, telling us that Caroline arrived "late to the first day of class, wearing a designer dress, not knowing who Lorrie Moore was but claiming she could recite the poems of Catullus in Latin." Not having heard of Lorrie Moore does not strike me as an especially black mark on the intellectual range of a college student, nor does knowing some Catullus seem wildly improbable for an Exeter graduate. But Natalie's essay "I Was Caroline Calloway" is a small masterpiece of a certain form: an aggrieved young woman's account of being repeatedly wronged, often by slights so minor that only someone very young could have nursed them so long and then decided that they demanded a public airing. One of her main beefs with Caroline is the amount of attention Caroline received from the world, when it was she, Natalie Beach, who had arrived on time and known about Lorrie Moore.

Both girls wanted to be writers, and they became fast friends, hanging out and getting high in Caroline's West Village apartment, where, Natalie reports, the walls were painted Tiffany blue and the place was filled with "fresh orchids and hardcovers," which is both an appealing way to decorate an apartment and a stylish way to describe it. You can already see, in this simple detail, how the girls could fuse together, one of them making a beautiful life, the other deeply attuned to its component parts.

Caroline admitted to Natalie that her heart had been broken when she was denied admission to Yale, which gave Natalie the inspiration for a gag gift. She was a New Haven townie, and her mother had once come across three plates stamped with the Yale crest discarded outside a campus building. Natalie took a Sharpie and wrote "Fuck Yale" on the back of each one, wrapped them up, and gave them to Caroline, who seemed pleased. But shortly thereafter, the plates disappeared from Caroline's apartment. Natalie says that Caroline said they'd been stolen, which was obviously not true, as nothing else from the apartment crammed with valuable items had been taken. Natalie was miffed, and remains so to this day. But there is no sentiment Caroline Calloway is less likely to hold than "Fuck Yale." Yale was the point; Harvard was the point; Cambridge was the point. Caroline once told Natalie that she would "rather die than go through life with an NYU alumni email address," which is a very Caroline thing to say. It showed her devotion to prestigious institutions, and it was also thoughtless and cutting. Natalie wasn't transferring; Natalie would have to make peace with a life lived in the shadow of a crappy email address.

Let's make one thing perfectly clear: Caroline Calloway is the kind of friend who, even if paired with a relative equal, could atomize your ego in less time than it takes to order a double macchiato. Natalie's fusing herself to Caroline was bound to end in her profound unhappiness. Caroline is self-involved, very pretty, able to bend strangers—especially male strangers—to her will; and Natalie, in her telling, is none of these things. Caroline is also very, very careless: with people's emotions, with her belongings, with the opportunities presented to her. But Natalie is the one who forced herself into Caroline's creative projects, out of envy and desire. She's been seething with jealousy for a long time.

Natalie took a semester abroad in London, at the end of which Caroline joined her for a holiday in Sicily. Natalie initially recalled the trip as fun, but later she read a journal entry that revealed it hadn't been such a good time. Reading her diary, Natalie "realized how bitter I'd been." She'd written that she wished "something bad would happen . . . a humiliation, like the one I feel always," concluding, "There has to be a price for getting everything you want. For never being embarrassed." Years later, the essay in *The Cut* was the price.

While Natalie was abroad, Caroline did something fateful: She started an Instagram account. Right away, Caroline realized that it could be a vehicle for magnifying herself and her talents to a larger world. As terrible as she would turn out to be at moneymakers such as delivering manuscripts and hosting workshops, Caroline had a deep and intuitive understanding of Instagram. She realized that it could be more than what people were then calling it: Twitter for people who couldn't read. She was far ahead of most in recognizing that the site allowed users to add long, novelistic captions to the images they posted. She was interested in becoming a writer and she was interested in herself—she was made for Instagram. She decided the account would serve as a venue for an extended work of creative nonfiction, and that the imminent start of her Cambridge education would be a perfect subject for it.

She paid for roughly 20,000 followers. Moreover, she was one of the early vanguard of users who understood that buying ads, if done correctly, could be a huge boost to an account. Imagining that her proposed subject would have particular appeal to the YA market, she bought ads on the fan accounts of successful YA books including *The Hunger Games* and *The Fault in Our Stars*.

Most important, she bought ads on Harry Potter fan sites. That series is based on the great British boarding-school books, such as Enid Blyton's beloved Malory Towers series and the novels of Angela Brazil, who all but invented the form. J. K. Rowling's stories built on that popular tradition by adding the element of wizardry. Soon, the world discovered the pleasures of reading about growing up within one of those historic, tradition-bound places, with their elaborate rituals, their formal robes, their generations-long sense of continuity. In writing about Cambridge, Caroline showed a mostly American audience that the dream world they had encountered in Rowling's series was not all invention and didn't end at age 18. Her account presented followers with a beautiful female protagonist beginning at a storied and ritual-laden English institution not at 12, but at 22.

A

This is what made Caroline Calloway's Instagram account famous: her Cambridge years, expressed as *Brideshead Revisited* meets *Twilight* meets *Vanity Fair* magazine circa 1988, when greed was good and having money was a golden superpower. She gave herself the persona of a rich, careless, happy American girl who falls utterly in love with Cambridge.

So here is Caroline, in ball gown after ball gown, sitting at candlelit dinners in great halls, her head inclined toward one handsome young man or another, or punting on the Cam wearing an orange gown and sunglasses and shielding her face from the sun with a pink parasol, a handsome young man in a dinner jacket sprawled at her feet. Here is the Henley Royal Regatta, and the Oxford Hunt Ball.

And here is the principal romance of the Cambridge years, Oscar, who opens his dormitory door to Caroline one morning, wearing only Ralph Lauren boxers, seeming to already know her, to have been waiting for her. And all of this—the languor with which she approaches her days, her apparent nonconcern about her future—takes her account out of time. Typically, an American girl who attends a top boarding school and then Cambridge is on the superhighway to becoming a "global leader," a leaner-inner, a person who drives herself every day to get to the top. But Caroline's attitude toward Cambridge, as presented on Instagram, is as relaxed as a pale hand trailing through the waters of the Cam.

She seems like a spoiled golden girl of yesteryear, someone whose life path and material comforts were so predestined that she could spend the days of her precious youth making flower crowns. She is in a dreamland of met desires, majoring in art history and writing her undergraduate thesis—if this were really a novel, not a writer in the world could have gotten this so exactly right—on the notebooks of Cecil Beaton.

But that is not the only thing that makes her Instagram account feel out of time. The other is that it is crammed full of ravishing images of great European paintings and architecture, as well as endless, admiring references to aristocrats—all without any attempt to place them within the contemporary concerns of race, class, and gender; all without any consideration of Europe as a malevolent and colonial force. Seeing an educated young person take in European art and culture with unconflicted admiration is so unusual that the first time I breezed through her account, I wondered if it was possibly an invention of someone from the "alt-light" world of young people who have taken about half of the red pill. But no, her politics turn out to be as doctrinaire as those of any other hyper-educated New York–dwelling millennial. It seems, simply, that she's the very last student to approach Western art not as the by-product of oppression, but only for its beauty, its power to move the viewer. She is eager to immerse herself only in the sensual experience of it; she is the Walter Pater of Instagram.

So here is *Girls After the Ball*, by József Borsos, and John Singer Sargent's little girls with paper lanterns and a Pompeii fresco. Here is a Hans Holbein portrait, and the July page of *Très Riches Heures*. Painting after painting— not the greatest hits from a survey course, but rather works that show some range and hint at her tastes. Here, too, are the Great European Ideas and the Great European Families. Here she is wondering if hoarding might run in a family, "like hemophilia in the House of Hanover, and insanity in the Hapsburgs?" And here she is seeking to comfort herself by tending to her own garden and keeping her mind on "the Voltarian sense of soul."

However unintentionally, she seems to be staging a one-girl defense of Western culture, territory she pretty much has to herself at this point. *The West! What a fantastic back catalog!*

To this day, she regularly posts works of art and pairs them with thoughtful and sensitive observations. It comes at you, perforce, interleaved with endless posts dedicated to her self-obsession; her various dramas; her endless, endless selfies. All of that is tedious. It's the art and her ideas about it that get my attention and elevate her intentions.

Taken all together, her account is a kind of madhouse, which suggests that Instagram is pretty good at exposing the range of a young person. There's the great Cambridge romance novel, the endless stories of hurt feelings and social triumphs, the selfies without number, and the glowing images of the greatest paintings and architecture in the history of the world—all of this is presented in the Instagram form, which is nonlinear, marked by short bursts of narration, and richly illustrated.

The 1990s introduced us to the idea that the "memoir" wasn't the sole province of presidents and dowagers, and that any 26-year-old woman with a boatload of problems and a humanities degree could write an engaging account of her experiences thus far. But the published book, as a medium, is perhaps too much and too little for the life and times of an extremely young person. Instagram, like Baby Bear's porridge, is just right. In this form, the past—which, let's face it, is a pretty slim chunk of time in the life of a 20-year-old—repeats itself, amends itself, inscribes new details on old stories; it's a form in which the triumphs and hurts of yesterday or yesteryear can be called up, reworked, reintroduced to the narrative as though they are as real and as present as anything happening in the actual moment. Just as important, the platform allows photographs to have equal weight with prose, which is essential for a young person who has grown up in the smartphone generation. All of it spools forward and backward, with no regard to linear time, like a postmodern novel.

A

But everything exacts a price, and Instagram is no different. It ends up flattening young women, taking whatever was original in them and slowly forcing it into the language and tropes of the site. In Cambridge, Caroline created someone out of time, sexually sophisticated but withholding of every secret detail. Lately, though, she is becoming like everyone else: She holds up her middle finger to the camera, posts about her great, "juicy" ass, decides that her signature phrase is "Suck my big fat cock." Yawn.

Moreover, the successful Instagram accounts of young women inevitably develop a common, unplanned, and dull theme: the emotional toll that the online haters exact from them and how to cope with it. Always, these young women choose the same three approaches and cycle through them during periods of duress. There's the badass: "Fuck people who don't understand me." There's the Judy Garland: "All I ever wanted to do was sing 'Somewhere Over the Rainbow.' All I ever wanted to do was make people happy." And there's the spreading of memes by professional uplifters. When Caroline began posting the sayings of Schlockmeister General Glennon Doyle, it was a low day for her account. Where was Cecil Beaton? Where, for that matter, was Voltaire?

The publication of Natalie's essay has been rich fodder for new content created by fans and toads, by journalists and tweeters. The two principals have been speaking to each other in oblique ways. To the *New York Times*, Natalie played the executioner's song—"I haven't been looking at her feed right now in part because I feel a deep guilt about causing her pain"—while also revealing that her inbox is so full of possibilities, she can hardly contend with it. And she offers Caroline a strange crumb of gratitude. "It's a small thing," she told the *Times*, "but Caroline was the one who introduced me to the man who did me the great honor of relieving me of my virginity. Which was very nice of her. And I'll be eternally grateful." Finding a man willing to take the virginity of a healthy, young NYU student hardly seems like one of the labors of Hercules.

As for Caroline, that Gatsby-like figure—the name changed to something less ethnic; the Oxbridge obsession; the conviction that you can transform your life and rewrite its origin story if you can just peg them to a few solid and impressive facts—she's been rocked by the events of the past weeks.

When her father died, she wasn't sure what to do. It had been so long since she'd known what to do about him. She ended up taking the train to Harvard, the only place the spirit of the man might linger. She met a boy and had "the most perfect date." She toured the archives of the newspaper, where she made a shocking discovery: Her father hadn't been "#2 at the *Crimson*." He'd only ever gotten a single letter to the editor published in the paper. But Caroline is quick on her feet in such matters; Caroline will never be daunted by an unwelcome truth.

"It turns out I misremembered," she tells us. "My Dad was second-in-command at *The Exonian*, Phillips Exeter Academy's student newspaper."

She went to a late-night party at the *Lampoon*, and then two new friends took her somewhere she wanted to go: Adams House, where her father had lived, and where there were no records to check, no mean nicknames to be told. She could be in the present, and she could conjure the past; and she could fuse the two and make them beautiful and perfect, a daughter's coda that could have come right out of Gatsby:

"He died in the house I grew up in, in debt, in pain, alone, surrounded by his hoarded mess. But in Adams House he was young, bright, and still hadn't done any of the things for which I have forgiven him."

As for Caroline herself, she's back in her cluttered studio apartment, where the art supplies and candles and paper cutouts threaten to overwhelm the place, still pumping out posts that trade extreme self-obsession with considered comments about art. The toads think the apartment is a hoarder's squat. The fans think it's a gem. Caroline wants all of them to lift their sights.

"Shoebox? Jewel box?" she asks rhetorically. Neither is right for this dreamer, this girl who has seen Venice and endured Falls Church.

"Sainte-Chapelle, anyone?"

THE MEDIA BOTCHED THE
COVINGTON CATHOLIC STORY

_____

January 2019

ON FRIDAY, JANUARY 18, a group of white teenage boys wearing MAGA hats mobbed an elderly Native American man on the steps of the Lincoln Memorial, chanting "Make America great again," menacing him, and taunting him in racially motivated ways. It is the kind of thing that happens every day—possibly every hour—in Donald Trump's America. But this time there was proof: a video. Was it problematic that it offered no evidence that these things had happened? No. What mattered was that it had happened, and that there was video to prove it. The fact of there being a video became stronger than the video itself.

The video shows a man playing a tribal drum standing directly in front of a boy with clear skin and lips reddened from the cold; the boy is wearing a MAGA hat, and he is smiling at the man in a way that is implacable and inscrutable. The boys around him are cutting up—dancing to the drumbeat, making faces at one another and at various iPhones, and eventually beginning to tire of whatever it is that's going on. Soon enough, the whole of the video's meaning seems to come down to the smiling boy and the drumming man. They are locked into something, but what is it?

Twenty seconds pass, then 30—and still the boy is smiling in that peculiar way. What has brought them to this strange, charged moment? From the short clip alone, it is impossible to tell. Because the point of the viral video was that it was proof of racist bullying yet showed no evidence of it, the boy quickly became the subject of rage and disgust. "I'd be ashamed and appalled if he was my son," the actress Debra Messing tweeted.

A second video also made the rounds. Shot shortly after the event, it consisted of an interview with the drummer, Nathan Phillips. There was something powerful about it, something that seemed almost familiar. It seemed to tell us an old story, one that's been tugging at us for years. It was a battered Rodney King stepping up to the microphones in the middle of the Los Angeles riots, asking, "Can we all get along? Can we get along?" It was the beautiful hippie boy putting flowers in the rifle barrels of military policemen at the March on the Pentagon.

In the golden hour at the Lincoln Memorial, the lights illuminating the vault, Phillips stands framed against the light of the setting sun, wiping tears from his eyes as he describes what has happened—with the boys, with the country, with land itself. His voice soft, unsteady, he begins:

> As I was singing, I heard them saying, "Build that wall, build that wall." This is indigenous land; we're not supposed to have walls here. We never did . . . We never had a wall. We never had a prison. We always took care of our elders. We took care of our children . . . We taught them right from wrong. I wish I could see . . . the [young men] could put that energy into making this country really great . . . helping those that are hungry.

It was moving, and it was an explanation of the terrible thing that had just happened—"I heard them saying, 'Build that wall.'" It was an ode to a nation's lost soul. It was also the first in a series of interviews in which Phillips would prove himself adept—far more so than the news media—at incorporating any new information about what had actually happened into his version of events. His version was all-encompassing, and he was treated with such patronizing gentleness by the news media that he was never directly confronted with his conflicting accounts.

When the country learned that Phillips was—in addition to being, as we were endlessly reminded, a "Native elder"—a veteran of the Vietnam War, the sense of anger about what had happened to him assumed new dimensions. That he had defended our country only to be treated so poorly by these MAGA-hatted monsters blasted the level of the boys' malevolence into outer space.

The journalist Kara Swisher found a way to link the horror to an earlier news event, tweeting:

> And to all you aggrieved folks who thought this Gillette ad was too much bad-men-shaming, after we just saw it come to life with those awful kids and their fetid smirking harassing that elderly man on the Mall: Go fuck yourselves.

You know the left has really changed in this country when you find its denizens glorifying America's role in the Vietnam War and lionizing the social attitudes of the corporate monolith Procter & Gamble.

Celebrities tweeted furiously, desperate to insert themselves into the situation in a flattering light. They adopted several approaches: old-guy concern about the state of our communities ("Where are their parents, where are their teachers, where are their pastors?": Joe Scarborough); dramatic professions of personal anguish meant to recenter the locus of harm from Phillips to the tweeter ("This is Trump's America. And it brought me to tears. What are we teaching our young people? Why is this OK? How is this OK? Please help me understand. Because right now I feel like my heart is living outside of my body": Alyssa Milano); and the inevitable excesses of the temperamentally overexcited: ("#CovingtonCatholic high school seems like a hate factory to me": Howard Dean).

By Saturday, the story had become so hot, and the appetite for it so deep, that some news outlets felt compelled to do some actual reporting. This was when the weekend began to take a long, bad turn for respected news outlets and righteous celebrities. Journalists began to discover that the viral video was not, in fact, the Zapruder film of 2019, and that there were other videos—lots and lots of them—that showed the event from multiple perspectives and that explained more clearly what had happened. At first the journalists and their editors tried to patch the revelations onto the existing story, in hopes that the whole thing would somehow hold together. CNN, apparently by now aware that the event had taken place within a complicating larger picture, tried to use the new information to support its own biased interpretation, sorrowfully reporting that early in the afternoon the boys had clashed with "four African American young men preaching about the Bible and oppression."

But the wild, uncontrollable internet kept pumping videos into the ether that allowed people to see for themselves what had happened.

The *New York Times*, sober guardian of the exact and the nonsensational, had cannonballed into the delicious story on Saturday, titling its first piece "Boys in 'Make America Great Again' Hats Mob Native Elder at Indigenous Peoples March."

But the next day it ran a second story, with the headline "Fuller Picture Emerges of Viral Video of Native American Man and Catholic Students."

How had the boys been demilitarized from wearers of "Make America Great Again" hats to "Catholic students" in less than 24 hours?

O, for a muse of fire.

It turned out that the "four African American young men preaching about the Bible and oppression" had made a video, almost two hours in length, and while it does not fully exonerate the boys, it releases them from most of the serious charges.

The full video reveals that there was indeed a Native American gathering at the Lincoln Memorial, that it took place shortly before the events of the viral video, and that during it the indigenous people had been the subject of a hideous tirade of racist insults and fantasies. But the white students weren't the people hurling this garbage at them— the young "African American men preaching about the Bible and oppression" were doing it. For they were Black Hebrew Israelites, a tiny sect of people who believe they are the direct descendants of the 12 tribes of Israel, and whose beliefs on a variety of social issues make Mike Pence look like Ram Dass.

The full video reveals that these kids had wandered into a Tom Wolfe novel and had no idea how to get out of it.

It seems that the Black Hebrew Israelites had come to the Lincoln Memorial with the express intention of verbally confronting the Native Americans, some of whom had already begun to gather as the video begins, many of them in Native dress. The Black Hebrew Israelites' leader begins shouting at them: "Before you started worshipping totem poles, you was worshipping the true and living God. Before you became an idol worshipper, you was worshipping the true and living God. This is the reason why this land was taken away from you! Because you worship everything except the most high. You worship every creation except the Creator—and that's what we are here to tell you to do."

A young man in Native dress approaches them and gestures toward the group gathering for its event. But the Black Hebrew Israelites mix things up by throwing some dead-white-male jargon at him—they are there because of "freedom of the speech" and "freedom of religion" and all that. The young man backs away. "You have to come away from your religious philosophy," one Black Hebrew Israelite yells after him.

A few more people in Native costume gather, clearly stunned by his tirade. "You're not supposed to worship eagles, buffaloes, rams, all types of animals," he calls out to them.

A

A Native woman approaches the group and begins to challenge its ideology, which prompts the pastor's coreligionists to thumb their Bibles for relevant passages from Proverbs and Ecclesiastes. He asks the woman why she's angry, and when she tells him that she's isn't angry, he responds, "You're not angry? You're not angry? I'm making you angry." The two start yelling at each other, and the speaker calls out to his associates for Isaiah 58:1.

Another woman comes up to him yelling, "The Bible says a lot of shit. The Bible says a lot of shit. The Bible says a lot of shit."

Black Hebrew Israelites believe, among other things, that they are indigenous people. The preacher tells a woman that "you're not an Indian. Indian means 'savage.'"

Men begin to gather with concerned looks on their faces. "Indian does not mean 'savage,'" one of them says reasonably. "I don't know where you got that from." At this point, most of the Native Americans who have surrounded—"mobbed"?—the preacher have realized what the boys will prove too young and too unsophisticated to understand: that the "four young African American men preaching about the Bible and oppression" are the kind of people you sometimes encounter in big cities, and the best thing to do is steer a wide berth. Most of them leave, exchanging amused glances at one another. But one of the women stays put, and she begins making excellent points, some of which stump the Black Hebrew Israelites.

It was heating up to be an intersectional showdown for the ages, with the Black Hebrew Israelites going head to head with the Native Americans. But when the Native woman talks about the importance of peace, the preacher finally locates a unifying theme, one more powerful than anything to be found in Proverbs, Isaiah, or Ecclesiastes.

He tells her there won't be any food stamps coming to reservations or the projects because of the shutdown, and then gesturing to his left, he says, "It's because of these . . . bastards over there, wearing 'Make America Great Again' hats."

The camera turns to capture five white teenage boys, one of whom is wearing a MAGA hat. They are standing at a respectful distance, with their hands in their pockets, listening to this exchange with expressions of curiosity. They are there to meet their bus home.

"Why you not angry at them?" the Black Hebrew Israelite asks the Native American woman angrily.

"That's right," says one of his coreligionists, "little corny-ass Billy Bob."

The boys don't respond to this provocation, although one of them smiles at being called a corny-ass Billy Bob. They seem interested in what is going on, in the way that it's interesting to listen to Hyde Park speakers.

The Native woman isn't interested in attacking the white boys. She keeps up her argument with the Black

Hebrew Israelites, and her line of reasoning is so powerful that it throws the preacher off track.

"She trying to be distracting," one of the men says. "She trying to stop the flow."

"You're out of order," the preacher tells the woman. "Where's your husband? Let me speak to him."

By now the gathering of Covington Catholic boys watching the scene has grown to 10 or 12, some of them in MAGA hats. They are about 15 feet away, and while the conflict is surely beyond their range of experience, it also includes biblical explication, something with which they are familiar.

"Don't stand to the side and mock," the speaker orders the boys, who do not appear to be mocking him. "Bring y'all cracker ass up here and make a statement." The boys turn away and begin walking back to the larger group.

"You little dirty-ass crackers. Your day coming. Your day coming . . . 'cause your little dusty asses wouldn't walk down a street in a black neighborhood, and go walk up on nobody playing no games like that," he calls after them, but they take no notice. "Yeah, 'cause I will stick my foot in your little ass."

By now the Native American ceremony has begun, and the attendees have linked arms and begun dancing. "They just don't know who they are," one of the Black Hebrew

Israelites says remorsefully to another. Earlier he had called them "Uncle Tomahawks."

The boys have given up on him. They have joined the larger group, and together they all begin doing some school-spirit cheers; they hum the stadium-staple opening bars of "Seven Nation Army" and jump up and down, dancing to it. Later they would say that their chaperones had allowed them to sing school-spirit songs instead of engaging with the slurs hurled by the Black Hebrew Israelites.

And then you hear the sound of drumming, and Phillips appears with several other drummers, all of them headed to the large group of boys. "Here come Gad!" says the Black Hebrew Israelite excitedly. His religion teaches that Native Americans are one of the 12 tribes of Israel, Gad. Apparently he thinks that his relentless attack on the Native Americans has led some of them to confront the white people. "Here come Gad!" he says again, but he is soon disappointed. "Gad not playing! He came to the rescue!" he says in disgust.

The drummers head to the boys, and keep playing. The boys, who had been jumping to "Seven Nation Army," start jumping in time to the drumming. Phillips takes a step toward the group, and then—as it parts to admit him—he walks into it. Here the Black Hebrew Israelites' footage is of no help, as Phillips has moved into the crowd.

Now we may look at the viral video—or, as a CNN chyron called it, the "heartbreaking viral video"—as well as the many others that have since emerged, none of which has so far revealed the boys to be chanting anything about a wall or about making America great again. Phillips keeps walking into the group, they make room for him, and then—the smiling boy. One of the videos shows him doing something unusual. At one point he turns away from Phillips, stops smiling, and locks eyes with another kid, shaking his head, seeming to say the word *no*. This is consistent with the long, harrowing statement that the smiling boy would release at the end of the weekend, in which he offered an explanation for his actions that is consistent with the video footage that has so far emerged, and revealed what happened to him in the 48 hours after Americans set to work doxing him and threatening his family with violence. As of this writing, it seems that the smiling boy, Nick Sandmann, is the one person who tried to be respectful of Phillips and who encouraged the other boys to do the same. And for this, he has been by far the most harshly treated of any of the people involved in the afternoon's mess at the Lincoln Memorial.

I recommend that you watch the whole of the Black Hebrew Israelites' video, which includes a long, interesting passage, in which the Covington Catholic boys engage in a mostly thoughtful conversation with the Black Hebrew Israelite preacher. Throughout the conversation, they disrespect him only once—to boo him when he says something vile about gays and lesbians. (Also interesting is the section at the very end of the video, in which—after the boys have left—the Black Hebrew Israelites are approached by some police officers. The preacher had previously spent time castigating police and "the penal code," so I thought this would be a lively exchange, but the Israelites treat the cops with tremendous courtesy and gratitude, and when they leave the pastor describes them as "angels." So let that be a lesson about the inadvisability of thinking you can predict how an exchange with a Black Hebrew Israelite will end up.)

I have watched every bit of video I can find of the event, although more keep appearing. I have found several things that various of the boys did and said that are ugly, or rude, or racist. Some boys did a tomahawk chop when Phillips walked into their group. There is a short video of a group that seems to be from the high school verbally harassing two young women as the women walk past it. In terms of the school itself, Covington Catholic High School apparently has a game-day tradition of students painting their skin black for "black-out days," but any attempt by the school to cast this as innocent fun is undercut by a photograph of a white kid in black body paint leering at a black player on an opposing team.

I would not be surprised if more videos of this kind turn up, or if more troubling information about the school emerges, but it will by then be irrelevant, as the elite media have botched the story so completely that

A

they have lost the authority to report on it. By Tuesday, the *New York Times* was busy absorbing the fact that Phillips was not, apparently, a Vietnam veteran, as it had originally reported, and it issued a correction saying that it had contacted the Pentagon for his military record, suggesting that it no longer trusts him as a source of reliable information.

How could the elite media—the *New York Times*, let's say—have protected themselves from this event, which has served to reinforce millions of Americans' belief that traditional journalistic outlets are purveyors of "fake news"? They might have hewed to a concept that once went by the quaint term "journalistic ethics." Among other things, journalistic ethics held that if you didn't have the reporting to support a story, and if that story had the potential to hurt its subjects, and if those subjects were private citizens, and if they were moreover minors, you didn't run the story. You kept reporting it; you let yourself get scooped; and you accepted that speed is not the highest value. Otherwise, you were the trash press.

At 8:30 yesterday morning, as I was typing this essay, the *New York Times* emailed me. The subject line was "Ethics Reminders for Freelance Journalists." (I have occasionally published essays and reviews in the *Times*). It informed me, inter alia, that the *Times* expected all of its journalists, both freelance and staff, "to protect the integrity and credibility of *Times* journalism." This meant, in part, safeguarding the *Times*'s "reputation for fairness and impartiality."

I am prompted to issue my own ethics reminders for the *New York Times*. Here they are: You were partly responsible for the election of Trump because you are the most influential newspaper in the country, and you are not fair or impartial. Millions of Americans believe you hate them and that you will casually harm them. Two years ago, they fought back against you, and they won. If Trump wins again, you will once again have played a small but important role in that victory.

THE DISHONESTY OF
THE ABORTION DEBATE

December 2019

IN 1956, TWO AMERICAN PHYSICIANS, J. A. Presley and
W. E. Brown, colleagues at the University of Arkansas
School of Medicine, decided that four recent admissions
to their hospital were significant enough to warrant a published report. "Lysol-Induced Criminal Abortion" appeared
in the journal *Obstetrics & Gynecology*. It describes four
women who were admitted to the hospital in extreme dis-
tress, all of them having had "criminal abortions" with
what the doctors believed to be an unusual agent: Lysol.
The powerful cleaner had been pumped into their wombs.
Three of them survived, and one of them died.

The first woman arrived at the hospital in a "hysterical
state." She was 32 years old, her husband was with her,
and she was in the midst of an obvious medical crisis: Her
temperature was 104 degrees, and her urine was "port-
wine" colored and contained extremely high levels of
albumin, indicating that her kidneys were shutting down.
Her husband eventually confessed that they had gone to
a doctor for an abortion two days earlier. Four hours after
admission, the woman became agitated; she was put in

restraints and sedated. Two hours after that, she began to breathe in the deep and ragged manner of the dying. An autopsy revealed massive necrosis of her kidneys and liver.

The second woman was 28 years old and bleeding profusely from her vagina. "After considerable questioning," she admitted that two days earlier, a substance had been injected into her womb by the same doctor who had treated the first patient. She was given a blood transfusion and antibiotics. Doctors performed a dilation and curettage, removing necrotic tissue that had a strong smell of phenol, then a main ingredient in Lysol. She survived.

The third woman was 35 and had been bleeding abnormally for two weeks. She told the physicians that her doctor had given her "a prescription for medicine," but she denied having had an abortion. She was given a blood transfusion and antibiotics, but did not improve. Her pelvic discharge smelled strongly of phenol. She was given a D&C, and a placenta was removed. She recovered.

The fourth patient was 18 years old and had come to the hospital because of unusual bleeding, cramping, and "a loss of water through the vagina"—probably the beginning of labor, brought on by an abortion. Shortly after being admitted, she spontaneously aborted a four-and-a-half-month fetus. Phenol was found in both the fetal and placental tissue. The girl recovered.

I have read many accounts of complications and deaths from the years when abortion was illegal in this country.

A

The subject has always compelled me, because my mother told me many times that when she was a young nurse at Bellevue Hospital in New York City, she had twice sat beside girls as they died from botched abortions. Both girls were interviewed by detectives, who demanded to know the abortionists' names, but both refused to reveal them. "They were too terrified," my mother always said. The Arkansas cases contain strikingly consistent aspects of such reports: The women seem to have waited a long time before getting help, and they tried not to admit they'd had abortions, hoping they could be treated without telling the truth. Abortionists—to use the term of that era—typically extracted three promises from the women who sought them out: They must keep the procedure a secret; they must never reveal the abortionist's name; and no matter what happened to them afterward, they must never contact him or her again.

What surprised me about the Arkansas doctors' account was their confidence that while "the methods and drugs used in performing criminal abortions are legion," Lysol was "one of the more rare abortifacients." To the contrary, Lysol was commonly used in abortions. This was a fact that millions of women knew via the oldest whisper network in the country, but that physicians— almost all of them male—would discover slowly, leaving behind a bread-crumb trail of reports like this one: based on recent admissions, and available only to other doctors who happened to pick up a particular issue of a particular journal.

In addition to medical reports, we find evidence of Lysol abortions in personal accounts—the actor Margot Kidder, for example, spoke powerfully about hers—and in testimony from criminal proceedings. Court records from 1946, for instance, tell the story of a 16-year-old California girl named Rebecca, who moved in with her sister-in-law to hide her pregnancy and to get an abortion. A local woman named Sophie agreed to perform it. She made a mixture of boiling water, Lysol, and soap; injected the hot fluid into Rebecca's uterus; and told her to walk around for two hours. In the middle of the night, the girl began having cramps that wouldn't let up; she delivered a "well-formed, eight-inch fetus," which her sister, Rayette, buried. Sophie returned the next day to collect the balance of her $25 fee. The girl was in distress but was given only aspirin. By that night, her symptoms had become intolerable, and Rayette brought her to the hospital. Sophie was later convicted and sent to prison; it's unclear whether Rebecca survived.

By the 1960s, doctors seemed to have realized that Lysol was in fact a commonly used abortifacient, one with particular dangers. In 1961, Dr. Karl Finzer of Buffalo, New York, published a paper in the *Canadian Medical Association Journal* titled "Lower Nephron Nephrosis Due

A

to Concentrated Lysol Vaginal Douches." He described two cases. One of the women died; the other survived. In 1969, two physicians, Robert H. Bartlett and Clement Yahia, published a paper in *The New England Journal of Medicine* titled "Management of Septic Chemical Abortion with Renal Failure." It included five case histories of women who had attempted abortions, two with Lysol. The doctors estimated that 200,000 to 1 million criminal abortions took place each year in America, and that in many parts of the country abortion was a leading cause of maternal death. Overall mortality for patients who had become septic from botched abortions and were admitted to a hospital was 11 to 22 percent, but for those whose abortions had been induced with soap or Lysol, the mortality rate was reportedly an astounding 50 to 66 percent. "These young women," the authors reported dispassionately, "are all potentially salvageable."

We will never know how many women had abortions via this method, or how many died because of it. Why was Lysol, with its strong, unpleasant smell and its corrosive effect on skin, so often used? Because its early formulation contained cresol, a phenol compound that induced abortion; because it was easily available, a household product that aroused no suspicion when women bought it; and because for more than three decades, Lysol advertised the product as an effective form of birth control, advising women to douche with it in diluted form after sex, thus powerfully linking the product to the notion of family planning.

In a seemingly endless series of advertisements published from the '20s through the '50s, the Lysol company told the same story over and over again: One woman or another had "neglected her feminine hygiene" and thereby rendered herself odious to her husband, leaving her "held in a web of indifference" and introducing "doubt" and "inhibitions" into their intimate life. It was illegal to advertise contraception nationally before 1977, so the Lysol ads performed a coy bit of misdirection—they said that if women didn't douche after sex, they would lose their "dainty," or "feminine," or "youthful" appeal. The implication was that sex made them stink, which revolted their husbands. However, women in the past knew what women of the present know: Having sex doesn't make a woman stink, and the only necessary items for keeping clean are soap and water.

Read with this in mind, the ads appear rife with coded references to the idea of contraception. One woman's doctor has told her "never to run such careless risks" and prescribed Lysol. Another is told by her doctor that failing to douche with Lysol could "lead to serious consequences." Many of the ads stress that Lysol works "even in the presence of mucous matter," a possible reference to the byproducts of intercourse; some promote the fact that it "leaves no greasy aftereffect," probably a reference to the vaginal jellies that some women used as birth control.

A doctor tells one woman, "It's foolish to risk your marriage happiness by being careless about feminine hygiene—even once!" This is the language of contraception: something that must be used every single time, that can lead to serious repercussions if skipped even once, that one should never be careless about. The "doubts" introduced to the marital lovemaking, and the "inhibitions," are not the result of stink; they are the outcome of there being no reliable form of birth control and the constant anxiety that sex could result in an unwanted pregnancy.

There are dozens of these ads on the internet, where they forever shock young feminists. I've seen so many of them that I thought I knew all of their tropes and euphemisms. But this summer I came across one that stopped me cold. It was a simple image of a very particular kind of female suffering. The woman in this ad was not caught in a web of indifference; she was not relieved because she had been prescribed Lysol by her doctor. The woman in this image has been "careless"; she is facing the "serious consequences."

In a single panel, we see a line drawing of the kind of middle-class white housewife who was a staple of postwar advertising, although invariably the products she was selling were of use and of interest to women of all socioeconomic classes and all races—this product in particular.

Her hair is brushed and shining, her nails are manicured, and she wears a wedding ring. But her head is buried in her hands, and behind her loom the pages of a giant calendar. Over her bowed head, in neat Palmer-method handwriting, is a single sentence: "I just can't face it again."

There's a whole world in that sentence. To be a woman is to bear the entire consequence of sex. And here is one woman bearing that consequence: a married woman— probably with other children, for this is a matter of "again"—who for whatever reason is at her breaking point.

What could make a married woman living during the great postwar Baby Boom unable to face one more pregnancy? Start making a list of the possible reasons, and you might never stop. Maybe she'd had terrible pregnancies and traumatic births and she couldn't go through another one. Maybe she had suffered terribly from postpartum depression, and she'd just gotten past it. Maybe her husband was an angry or violent man; maybe he had a tendency to blame her when she got pregnant. Maybe she had finally reached the point in her life when her youngest was in school and she had a few blessed hours to herself each day, when she could sit in the quiet of her house and have a cup of coffee and get her thoughts together. And maybe—just maybe—she was a woman who knew her own mind and her own life, and who knew very well when something was too much for her to bear.

A

The fictional woman with her head in her hands made me think of a real woman who died as a result of using Lysol to control her fertility: the 32-year-old woman in the Arkansas report whose husband took her to the hospital, where she soon died. Given the era and given that she was 32, there's a fair chance that the couple had been married for at least a few years; there's also a pretty good chance they already had children. For whatever reason, she just couldn't face it again. She tried to do something to save herself—because when you can't face something, there is no other choice. And she paid for it with her life.

THE FIRST TIME I SAW one of the new 3D ultrasounds of a fetus in utero, I wasn't entirely sure what I was looking at. It wasn't anything like the black-and-white images I was used to seeing. It looked otherworldly, like we'd finally made contact with a planet we've always wanted to reach. In part it was the color, that glowing shade of amber that doesn't suggest anything medical or technological. It calls to mind something almost ancient, something that suggests the beginning of all things. It reminded me, both in color and somehow in meaning, of the earliest photographs of the bog people of Northern Europe, a phenomenon that had absorbed my attention when I was very young. Those ancient and particular faces, those people you could easily have picked out of a crowd, buried deep in the peat for more than 2,000 years, keeping their secrets, slumbering. When farmers cutting turf began discovering them in the 1950s, they were so perfectly preserved that the men assumed they had uncovered the remains of very recent murder victims, not the bodies of people who had lived before the time of Christ. And that was the shocking thing about the bog people: They were so clearly like us, so obviously human and individual.

These sonograms are so richly detailed that many expectant mothers pay to have one made in a shopping-mall studio, much in the spirit in which they might bring the baby to a portrait studio. They are one thing and one thing only: baby pictures. Had they been available when I was pregnant, I would definitely have wanted one. When you're pregnant, you are desperate to make contact. You know he's real because of the changes in your own body; eventually you start to feel his. The first kicks are startling and exciting, but even once they progress so far that you can see an actual foot glancing across your belly and then disappearing again, he's still a mystery, still engaged in his private work, floating in the aquatic chamber within you, more in touch with the forces that brought him here than with life as it is lived on the other side.

For a long time, these images made me anxious. They are proof that what grows within a pregnant woman's body is a human being, living and unfolding according to a timetable that has existed as long as we have. Obviously,

A

it would take a profound act of violence to remove him from his quiet world and destroy him.

"Most abortions happen in the first trimester," a very smart and very kind friend reassured me. I didn't need to worry about those detailed images of babies—by the time they had grown to such recognizably human proportions, most of them were well past the stage of development in which the majority of abortions take place. And I held on to that comforting piece of information, until it occurred to me to look at one of those images taken at the end of the first trimester. I often wish I hadn't.

A picture of a 12-week fetus is a Rorschach test. Some people say that such an image doesn't trouble them, that the fetus suggests the possibility of a developed baby but is far too removed from one to give them pause. I envy them. When I see that image, I have the opposite reaction. I think: *Here is one of us; here is a baby.* She has fingers and toes by now, eyelids and ears. She can hiccup—that tiny, chest-quaking motion that all parents know. Most fearfully, she is starting to get a distinct profile, her one and only face emerging. Each of these 12-week fetuses bears its own particular code: this one bound to be good at music; that one destined for a life of impatience, of tap, tap, tapping his pencil on the desk, waiting for recess.

What I can't face about abortion is the reality of it: that these are human beings, the most vulnerable among us, and we have no care for them. How terrible to know that in the space of an hour, a baby could be alive—his heart beating, his kidneys creating the urine that becomes the amniotic fluid of his safe home—and then be dead, his heart stopped, his body soon to be discarded.

The argument for abortion, if made honestly, requires many words: It must evoke the recent past, the dire consequences to women of making a very simple medical procedure illegal. The argument against it doesn't take even a single word. The argument against it is a picture.

This is not an argument anyone is going to win. The loudest advocates on both sides are terrible representatives for their cause. When women are urged to "shout your abortion," and when abortion becomes the subject of stand-up comedy routines, the attitude toward abortion seems ghoulish. Who could possibly be proud that they see no humanity at all in the images that science has made so painfully clear? When anti-abortion advocates speak in the most graphic terms about women "sucking babies out of the womb," they show themselves without mercy. They are not considering the extremely human, complex, and often heartbreaking reasons behind women's private decisions. The truth is that the best argument on each side is a damn good one, and until you acknowledge that fact, you aren't speaking or even thinking honestly about the issue. You certainly aren't going to convince anybody. Only the truth has the power to move.

And here is one truth: No matter what the law says, women will continue to get abortions. How do I know? Because in the relatively recent past, women would allow strangers to brutalize them, to poke knitting needles and wire hangers into their wombs, to thread catheters through their cervices and fill them with Lysol, or scalding-hot water, or lye. Women have been willing to risk death to get an abortion. When we made abortion legal, we decided we weren't going to let that happen anymore. We were not going to let one more woman arrive at a hospital with her organs rotting inside of her. We accepted that we might lose that growing baby, but we were not also going to lose that woman.

I thought about many women while I was writing this essay. The two girls my mother had watched die, all the women who endured Lysol abortions. But I also thought about a man: the husband of that 32-year-old woman who died in Arkansas, so long ago. It was an act of courage—a rare one—for him to bring her in himself, and to stay with her. Both of them had conspired in a criminal activity. How can we calculate that man's misery? Imagine him sitting in the hospital waiting room, an obscene pantomime of the times he had likely sat in a very different kind of waiting room, as his children were being born. Imagine the disdain with which he would have been regarded by many of the nurses and doctors. It would have been impossible, during those wretched hours, to try to explain to them that his wife had said she just couldn't face it again, and that he had tried to help her. At some point he would have been told that she was gone and also that there would have to be an autopsy. And then, when nothing else was left to do, no other form to sign and no other question to answer, imagine him getting in the car and making the terrible drive back to his house so that he could tell his children that their mother was never coming home again.

A

MEGHAN MARKLE DIDN'T DO THE WORK

March 2021

LOOKS LIKE PRINCE HARRY married a girl just like the one who married dear old Dad. We recognized all of it: the desperate unhappiness, the adoration of the masses, the beautiful clothes worn beautifully—but especially the easy and immediate way of reaching out to commoners and blessing them with the life-changing gift of her attention. He found—and then gave to us, the grateful public—another Diana. And Meghan Markle more than repaid the palace for her admission to the golden circle. She captured the affection of the entire world, she pumped up interest in the royals, and she had much to offer, all of it gladly given. Like Diana, she had the power to help the Royal Family survive a major challenge to its relevance. But, once again, a talented and life-giving outsider was rejected by the host organism.

In the couple's interview with Oprah Winfrey, Meghan looked poised and thoughtful, and managed to make her series of shocking revelations seem reluctantly tendered, a hostile witness having the terrible truth pulled out of her, much more in sorrow than in anger. When Harry was allowed into the conversation, he sat beside his wife looking like he'd been shot from a cannon. Before he met Meghan, he was a prince of Europe—almost a crown prince—a young man whose life was part of a continuation from Excalibur to Afghanistan, where he fought with valor in the manner of Prince Hal finding within himself Henry V. Now, however, he is like Antonio: tempest-tossed and thrown up upon the wide beaches of the brave new world. Once, he led men into battle, as his forebears had done for generations. Now he is a Californian with a Spotify deal, charged with thinking up some podcasts, which could be a heavy lift. For Harry, the situation is evolving.

Diana joined the Royal Family when the operation was at a low ebb and somewhat imperiled. She signed up in 1981, when the grim realities of the 1970s showed no sign of abating. That decade had been a time of strikes and large-scale unemployment, and young people were disillusioned with many things, not least of them the notion of a family of magical creatures who must be carted around in golden carriages at government expense. In 1977, the Queen celebrated her Silver Jubilee, which touched the hearts of many Britons, especially those who had been young during the Blitz. To them she represented courage, continuity, and endurance. To the young, in the midst of the punk movement and a profound sense of alienation from the country's elite, she represented something very

A

different. They wore STUFF THE JUBILEE badges, and the same year, the Sex Pistols delivered the imperishable *Never Mind the Bollocks, Here's the Sex Pistols,* with its famous anthem, "God Save the Queen":

God save the queen
The fascist regime
They made you a moron
A potential H bomb

God save the queen
She ain't no human being
And there's no future
In England's dreaming

Don't be told what you want
Don't be told what you need

The album was a working-class yelp of frustration at the bollocks, that is to say the rubbish, all the things that weren't working in England—the ridiculous Royal Family very much among them. But then, just a year into the new and potentially anti-monarchist decade: Diana. For someone joining the family at the height of the punk movement's hatred of the monarchy, she shouldn't have been such an immediate hit. She was the daughter of an earl who lived in Althorp, a grand pile located on a 13,000-acre estate, the Spencer family's home since 1508. Her first childhood home, Park House, was a short drive from Sandringham, the Queen's country home, where Diana spent an unhappy portion of many unhappy Christmas mornings. Diana had attended a Swiss finishing school, and her father bought her a fashionable flat when she moved to London, where she became a member of the Sloane Rangers—its beau ideal, actually—a group of well-heeled, sophisticated Londoners. A perfect fit for the fascist regime, or so it might have seemed.

But that's not how it played. Not by a mile. With the announcement of her engagement to Prince Charles—her a naive 19, him a jaded 32—she instantly became a global celebrity, on her way to becoming the most known and most loved woman in the world. She didn't seem like the rest of the royals. She was painfully shy, and she was afraid of the press. She hadn't worked in the kind of Sloane Ranger patronage job she could have had in a second—at Sotheby's, or a PR firm or fashion magazine. She had worked in a kindergarten and as a nanny; she had cleaned her sister's flat on the weekends, for one pound an hour. She was the lonely child of a terrible divorce, which might have led to her great sympathy for children.

She was also a girl without "a history," as people would say, meaning she was assumed to have been a virgin, a girl whose head was filled with romantic fantasies and who had imagined that she was bound for an enchanted life. At first the fantasies seemed plausible: She was borne

A

forward on a giant tide of goodwill and international excitement to her bombastic, category-crushing wedding. There was an actual glass coach, a wedding dress with a 25-foot train, and a honeymoon on the royal yacht.

But Charles, of course, never left Camilla Parker Bowles, and soon enough Diana was embittered. She had revived people's fondness for the silly old monarchy and its endless nonsense, but what were her thanks? Her husband was MIA and her in-laws thought of her as troubled and childish. And soon she was no longer an impressionable teenager. She was someone who wielded tremendous power, who had great feeling for those who were suffering, but who had also become manipulative and narcissistic, vengeful and shallow. When she decided to unload both barrels on the Royal Family, first to the journalist Andrew Morton, the author of *Diana: Her True Story—In Her Own Words*, and then to the broadcaster Martin Bashir in an explosive television interview, she scorched the earth. She told Bashir that "the establishment," meaning the palace, couldn't stand her. The reason for this, she said—sounding much like Meghan Markle would nearly 30 years later—was that "I don't go by a rule book, because I lead from the heart, not the head . . . Someone's got to go out there and love people and show it." She would never be the Queen of England, she understood, but she would instead be "the queen of people's hearts." When she was killed two years later, the

Queen's apparent indifference to the nation's wild grief almost threatened to overturn the monarchy. Only when Elizabeth acknowledged the loss—flying the flag at Buckingham Palace at half-mast; returning to London from Balmoral Castle, where she had been on holiday; and meeting with mourners outside the gates of Buckingham Palace—was a crisis averted.

LIKE DIANA, Meghan entered the Royal Family at a time when it faced a considerable challenge to its longevity, one that she was uniquely capable of forestalling. In 1997, Prime Minister Tony Blair's Labour government passed an act that would permanently change the face and character of the United Kingdom, something that the writer and social critic Benjamin Schwarz called the country's "most profound social transformation since the Industrial Revolution." In an effort, apparently, to make the UK a full participant in the modern, globalized world, the government radically relaxed immigration policies, making it much easier for people to settle there. It initiated a wave of mass immigration to the country, which continues to this day. As Schwarz noted in his essential essay, "Unmaking England," in 2014 "636,000 migrants came to live in Britain, and 27 percent of births in Britain were to foreign-born mothers." The majority of the immigrants since 1997 were from Pakistan, India, Bangladesh, Somalia, and Nigeria. The result is that Britain, of all

A

places, is becoming one of the most multiethnic, multira-cial, and culturally diverse countries in the world—yet a monarchical structure remains within it that is and has always been 100 percent white. Before Meghan, thou-sands of English girls of color harbored the same princess dreams that white English girls had harbored for centu-ries. But when they saw pictures of the royals on the Buckingham Palace balcony, at their weddings and spe-cial events, and during the exciting moments when they presented their new babies to the world, they didn't see a single person who looked like them. They saw a family that, as Stephen Colbert put it, was a "medieval selective breeding program."

Meghan placed an oxygen mask on the monarchy, offering the potential to future-proof the institution for at least a couple more decades. Suddenly, a beautiful mixed-race woman was having the enchanted wedding, emerg-ing from an ancient chapel under an enormous bower of flowers, and then riding off in an open coach, with her prince beside her. Like Diana, she had the magic touch, a preternatural ability to make a powerful connection with people, in even just the moment or two of encountering them on a rope line. Crowds appeared wherever she went; she was loved.

In October 2019, Meghan and Harry made an official visit to South Africa. Meghan was received with adulation and great excitement, and this was evidence that she was the best thing that could have happened to the Royal Family, making it relevant and modern and respected by a new generation. In Cape Town's Nyanga township, she visited a human-rights organization and made a speech to a large group of women. She began it this way:

> While I am here with my husband as a member of the Royal Family, I want you to know that for me, I am here with you as a mother, as a wife, as a woman, as a woman of color, and as your sister. I am here, and I am here for you.

When I watched the video of the speech, I thought, *This woman is going to single-handedly save the British monarchy.*

But it turned out that visit was really the end of things. In a documentary about the trip, *Harry and Meghan: An African Journey*, a reporter asked Meghan whether she was "OK," and she took a long time to answer. "It's hard," she said at last, "and I don't think anyone could understand that. But in all fairness I had no idea." She said that when she had gotten engaged, her American friends had told her that was wonderful news, but her British friends had said, "I'm sure he's great. But you shouldn't do it, because the British tabloids will destroy your life." And then she said that for a long time she had told Harry, "It's not enough to just survive something. That's not the point of life." She could have been Diana talking about leading

A

from the heart, about the way that unchecked suffering can hollow you out. For his part, Harry told the reporter that he fretted about history repeating itself—his unhappy wife following in the footsteps of his unhappy mother, with devastation to come.

And all of this led, strangely enough, to Montecito, California, which is paradise on Earth, an enclave of very rich people living very enviable lives under the clean Santa Barbara sunshine, where the air is perfumed with orange blossoms, lavender, and rosemary. It led to Meghan's sitting down with Oprah for a TV interview in the Edenic garden of a pleasure palace midway between Oprah's Montecito pleasure palace and her own, and it led to her narrowing her eyes, looking at Oprah, and letting them have it back there in England.

Some viewers tuned in not understanding that Meghan is an extremely accomplished person, that she had not arrived in the Royal Family with only a B-list television show to her credit. Not at all. She had gone to Northwestern University, where she'd studied international relations and theater—probably the perfect combination of subjects for her future role as Harry's wife—and she had done an internship at the American embassy in Argentina. She had planned a life in the Foreign Service, although she did not pass the notoriously hard exam. In 2015, she was invited to speak about feminism at the United Nations, and in 2016, she traveled to Rwanda, Delhi, and Mumbai to promote World Vision's Clean Water Campaign. In short, she was hardly an L.A. starlet who got lucky and landed a series but had little else to show for herself. She's smart. Next to poor Harry, she's a Rhodes Scholar.

The interview began with the two women sitting across from each other under a pergola, making a convincing appearance of not knowing each other very well, even though they have a history. Oprah befriended Meghan early on, and saw the ways that she and Harry were suffering. Long before Harry and Meghan left England, Oprah and Harry had begun working together on a docuseries about mental health. So Meghan felt very safe—and was very safe—talking with Oprah and, in her measured and calculated way, plunging the knife into her in-laws' hearts.

The problems had begun about six months after the wedding; that was when things began to turn, when the tabloids decided to create a narrative. They had written that shortly before the wedding, Meghan had made Prince William's wife, Kate, cry in a dustup over flower-girl dresses, but that wasn't at all what had happened! Not at all! What had happened was that Kate had made *Meghan* cry about the flower-girl dresses. But Kate had made things right. Kate had behaved the way Meghan would have behaved if she had been in the wrong—although she had in no way been in the wrong—by apologizing and sending flowers. The palace should have protected her; the palace should have made a correction. But it had done nothing.

A

The palace was willing to lie to protect others in the family, but not "to tell the truth to protect" Meghan and Harry.

Meghan suggested during the two-hour interview that one of the chief acts of cruelty perpetrated against the couple had been the palace's refusal to "protect" them from the lies of the press. It did not seem to occur to her that the palace has no ability to protect its members from the tabloids, and that a story as inconsequential as tears shed over a flower girl's dress was best starved of oxygen, not inflamed by correction. Diana was killed because the palace couldn't control the tabloid press, and Prince Andrew had to be taken out of rotation because the papers kept the story of his involvement with Jeffrey Epstein alive week after week.

With the calumny of the flower-girl dresses cleared up, it was time to roll a piece of previously recorded tape, featuring Meghan, Harry, and Oprah squeezed into the young couple's chicken coop, which is populated with "rescue chickens." (Meghan: "I just love rescuing.") What was the best thing about their new life? Oprah asked from inside the coop. The chance "to live authentically," Meghan said, as though she and Harry were mucking out stables in Hertfordshire, not tending to rescue chickens on a $15 million estate. "It's so basic," she continued, "but it's really fulfilling. Just getting back down to basics."

Cut to the pergola. The couple's case against the Crown was that the Royal Family had not protected them from the tabloids, had stopped paying Harry—had "cut me off," he said, in the particular expression of shocked trust-funders the world over whenever Daddy decides: enough!—and had not provided any help when Meghan found herself so unhappy that she was having suicidal thoughts. The parents were also shocked by apparent concerns about how dark their future babies would be—a revolting development, but hardly a surprising one.

Part of Meghan's problem, it turned out, was her naïveté about the workings of the Royal Family, which she had assumed would be similar to the workings of celebrity culture. What was she, Meghan Markle, a simple girl from Los Angeles, to have understood about such an institution as the British? How was she to know that Elizabeth II, by the Grace of God, of the United Kingdom of Great Britain and Northern Ireland and of her other realms and territories Queen, Head of the Commonwealth, Defender of the Faith, was in any way different from the Lady of Gaga? One wonders whether her study of foreign service and international relations, her internship at the American embassy in Argentina, and her work with the UN might have clued her in to the fact that a whole world exists beyond the Jamba Juice on La Brea and the set of *Deal or No Deal*, on which she had once been one of the beautiful "suitcase girls." Apparently, they had not.

She told Oprah that she had never even Googled her future husband's name—a remark that united the

A

viewing world in hilarity, time zone by time zone. It was an assertion that strained credulity, but it was necessary to her contention that she'd had no idea that the Windsors had not, as we now say, "done the work" when it came to exploring their own racial biases. Had she herself done some work by punching her beloved's name into a search engine, she would have understood that she was not marrying the most racially conscious person on the planet. She would have seen pictures of him dressed as a Nazi at a costume party (his great-granduncle—briefly Edward VIII—had palled around with Adolf Hitler) and a videotape of him introducing a fellow cadet as "our little Paki friend." The Palace said that "Prince Harry used the term without any malice and as a nickname about a highly popular member of his platoon." But the palace had no good explanation for why Harry introduced another cadet in the video by saying, "It's Dan the Man. Fuck me, you look like a raghead."

BUT IT WAS MARKLE'S piety regarding the British Commonwealth and her possible relationship to it that revealed the essential incoherence of her case against the monarchy. For some reason she seemed to think that representing the British monarchy to the countries it had colonized was valorous. This group of countries, she told Oprah, is "60, 70 percent . . . people of color." Absolutely true. But what force brought these nations together? And why is this institution, composed of 54 countries, headed by—of all people—the Queen of England?

The English relationship to the "commonwealth" is a natural (or unnatural) connection to the British empire. Overwhelmingly, these are the countries that were colonized, exploited, and subjected to ruinous campaigns of violence and ethnic cleansing perpetrated by the British in the name not merely of country, but of the specific family Meghan chose to join. And her desire had been to become a special emissary to this confederation of countries as a representative of the Crown, as a standard bearer of a foreign power historically responsible for many of the specific miseries that exist in these places to this very day. Britain's eager participation in the notorious "Scramble for Africa" is directly responsible for the exploitation of natural resources in many parts of that continent. And that's the team she wanted to represent? Meghan Markle: defender of the Queen's "realms and territories."

The best thing the Royal Family could do for the former colonies would be to send money and stay away.

This matter had been left unaddressed by the time Harry arrived under the pergola—a bit flushed, obviously pained, and by no means as comfortable with the complicated new narrative as was his wife—and started answering questions. He revealed that he is estranged from his father, who at some point stopped taking his calls; that he loves his brother to bits, but that this relationship is also strained; that his adored grandmother had disinvited him and Meghan to lunch; and that when Netflix approached the couple with a deal, it was a stroke of luck, because "we hadn't thought about it." When they arrived in Los Angeles, cut off financially and stranded with only the funds left to Harry by his mother (and Meghan's money from her television work), they had been forced to huddle like refugees in Tyler Perry's mansion, allowing the superstar to pay for their security.

But more than any of this—more than Diana's sad life and tragic death, more than Meghan's disappointment at discovering that the Windsors aren't devotees of critical race theory, more than the rescue chickens and the Spotify deal and even the Montecito mansion—the main takeaway from Oprah's interview with Meghan and Harry was that it was spectacular television. Minute-for-minute excellent television. Oprah is one of the most famous people in the world; Meghan is an enormous celebrity. They both looked beautiful, and the setting was a garden of such exquisiteness that most of us will never lay eyes on its likeness outside of television or the movies. But what they were doing was talking about something most women have talked about with other women: in-law problems. They were on the grounds of an estate, but they could have been on the sidelines of a T-ball game or at a girls' night out, or waiting for the subway. The father-in-law was a prick; the brother's wife was a real pain and hadn't done anything to reduce bridal anxieties before the wedding; the grandmother was a doll, but too easily exploited by the nursing-home staff. They were loaded, but they had cut off a favored son when he'd most needed the money. Meghan had, in fact, realized the highest aspiration of many married people: She had convinced her spouse that his entire family was a bunch of losers. (Harry, on life before meeting Meghan: "I was trapped, but I didn't know I was trapped.") She had plucked him out of its bosom and made herself and their child his only true family. She was—depending on your point of view—either a virago or an icon.

Nothing is as galvanizing and unifying as an episode of appointment television in which a hugely famous female broadcaster delivers an exclusive interview with another hugely famous celebrity who is in the midst of what is essentially a personal drama.

I was reminded of Diane Sawyer's 1995 interview with Lisa Marie Presley and Michael Jackson soon after the pair's marriage, an event that had closely followed accusations that he was a child molester. Had she been worried about the charges? Asked him about the charges before marrying him?

"I've seen these children. They don't let him go to the bathroom without running in there with him."

And of Barbara Walters's 1999 interview with Monica Lewinsky. Why had she flashed her thong at Bill Clinton?

"It was saying, 'I'm interested, too. I'll play.'"

And Emily Maitlis's 2020 interview with Prince Andrew. Why had he stayed in Jeffrey Epstein's mansion after Epstein had been implicated in a massive sex-trafficking scheme?

"My judgment was probably colored by my tendency to be too honorable."

These were questions about marriage and crimes against women and sex between powerful men and impressionable young women. They were conversations among famous people, but they were also conversations among all of us: the world's women. They took the most elemental and baleful female conditions—sex and marriage, motherhood, and the ever-present threat of sexual danger—and transformed them into glossy television events. They gave us the kinds of details in which women—even the most intellectual and high-minded women—take an enduring interest, and they gave us an instant way to talk about them with one another.

I had an unpleasant medical procedure a few days after the Oprah special, but I was so focused on my nurse's opinion of the show (surprisingly anti-Meghan) that I hardly noticed the pain. I had forced my sons and husband to watch the interview with me, and when Oprah reminded Meghan that when you marry a person, you are also marrying that person's family, I cried out, "That's right!" The things women care about will always be with us, and the way women work through them is not to drop ordnance on Afghanistan. It's to find one another, put on the kettle or open the wine, and talk.

At the end of the interview, Harry sat beside Meghan, still looking a bit stunned, a bit unsure what was happening to him in this new life. Looking, in fact, a bit like a rescue chicken. Oprah asked him if Meghan had "saved him."

"Yeah, she did," he said. "Without question, she saved me."

Meghan reached out her hand and touched his arm, stopping him from going on.

"I would . . . I would . . ." she said, trying to locate the right note, trying perhaps to avoid the impression that her husband was one more chicken in her coop. *She* hadn't done the rescuing, she said—Harry had. It was Harry who had "certainly saved my life and saved all of us."

And Harry sat there beside her, 7,000 miles from home, in the land of rich Californians and Meyer lemons and eucalyptus trees trailing Spanish moss. He had plighted his troth to this unexpected and very beautiful woman; he had hurt his grandmother, and alienated his father and his only brother. He had thought that having Bishop Michael Bruce Curry deliver the homily at his wedding would reverse a thousand years of English racial attitudes, but he had been wrong about that. He was a combat veteran, a prince, the grandson, great-grandson, and great-great-grandson of English monarchs, and now he was going to have to think up some podcasts.

A

AMERICA'S FIRE SALE: GET SOME FREE SPEECH WHILE YOU CAN

August 2022

TWO YEARS AGO, a friend emailed me: Some writers were composing an open letter to appear in *Harper's*; it would address the growing threats to freedom of expression in this country. Did I want to read and possibly sign it? I read it and said to myself, *This is going to be a shitstorm of biblical proportions*, and wrote to my friend, "In."

Of course I was in. I have shown up for free expression when it was a major cause of the left, and I show up for it now that it has become a cause of the right. Freedom doesn't belong to a political party, and it's not the tool of the powerful; it's the tool of the powerless.

The letter came out, and in the small, bitter, vengeful worlds of journalism and publishing—we're a fun crowd—it was a festival of freedom of expression, a gathering of like-minded antagonists from the mighty to the dweeby. Someone named Richard Kim, who was then the enterprise director of *HuffPost*, tweeted (enterprisingly), "OK, I did not sign THE LETTER when I was asked 9 days ago because I could see in 90 seconds that it was fatuous, self-important drivel." (It was the *I also got into Cornell* of tweets: *Of course I think it's gross, but I want you to know I was asked*.)

Later in the week, about 150 writers and academics signed an open letter that appeared on Substack, "A More Specific Letter on Justice and Open Debate." They expressed a widely held, emerging idea about freedom of expression, which is that it cannot be considered without a coequal consideration of the issue of power. How could the *Harper's* signers have a rational discussion about free speech without a consideration of "the marginalized voices [who] have been silenced for generations in journalism, academia, and publishing"? The Substack writers observed that "Black, brown, and LGBTQ+ people—particularly Black and trans people—can now critique elites publicly and hold them accountable socially, and this was the signers' real concern."

The letter said that "the intellectual freedom of cis white intellectuals has never been under threat en masse" (To the memory hole, Mr. Solzhenitsyn!), and characterized the *Harper's* signers as a group of writers that has "never faced serious consequences—only momentary discomfort."

A week ago, one of *Harper's* signers, Salman Rushdie, experienced some of that momentary discomfort when he was nearly eviscerated on a sun-dappled Friday morning at the Chautauqua Institution. Rushdie signed the

Harper's letter, and I wondered why its critics hadn't allowed themselves a little carve-out where he was concerned, given that (a) he has been the most persecuted writer in the world for the past 30 years, and (b) it would be a bad look if someone tried to collect the $3 million bounty on his head in relative proximity to the "never faced serious consequences" claim.

SOON AFTER THE ATTACK, another writer who had signed the *Harper's* letter, J. K. Rowling, tweeted out the news about Rushdie, calling it "horrifying," and in short order received a serious death threat. A Twitter account called @MeerAsifAziz1—which had earlier praised the supreme leader of Iran and posted about the possible destruction of Israel, and that morning had called Rushdie's attacker a "revolutionary"— replied to Rowling: "Don't worry you are next."

@MeerAsifAziz1 does not strike one as the kind of person dedicated to trans rights, so what could he possibly have against Rowling? Gryffindor scarf on back order? Theme-park Butterbeer just nasty? I think the impulse was probably more in line with a union action—whenever writers are being threatened and attacked, you can count on jihadist solidarity.

The most important tweet was posted by PEN America, the organization that, for 100 years, has protected writers' freedom of expression: "We can think of no comparable incident of a public attack on a literary writer on American soil." But lately PEN has had to resist pressure from some of its members to abandon its mission. After the *Charlie Hebdo* massacre in 2015, the organization announced that it would be conferring a special award for courage on the survivors. This distressed 250 of its members, who signed a shameful open letter (if you're a writer and haven't signed an open letter, you need to call your agent). They said they were not clear—not clear at all—on the "criteria" used in making the decision to confer the prize.

I think the criteria probably had to do with surviving a massacre that left their colleagues' brains and blood pooled on the office floor, and the day after that announcing they would put out the next week's issue on time.

The letter chided the decision makers for forgetting that "the inequities between the person holding the pen and the subject fixed on paper by that pen cannot, and must not, be ignored." I'm a little more concerned with the person holding the knife.

PEN still gave the award to *Charlie Hebdo*—all honor to them. But some members who'd opposed it made their displeasure known in a stunning way: *They didn't go to the gala*. No dinner jacket, no tuna tartare at the Museum of Natural History, no making or enjoying of writerly witticisms. Just a bit of leftover prime beef, microwaved and eaten—to make the sacrifice as bitter as possible—off a TV tray.

ONE WRITER WHO SIGNED the *Harper's* letter was not just a member of PEN America; she was—and is—one of its trustees: Jennifer Finney Boylan. But on publication day, she freaked out. With trembling hands, she typed her own ransom note:

> I did not know who else had signed that letter. I thought I was endorsing a well-meaning, if vague, message against internet shaming. I did know Chomsky, Steinem, and Atwood were in, and I thought, good company. The consequences are mine to bear. I am so sorry.

Frederick Douglass said, "I would unite with anybody to do right and with nobody to do wrong." Boylan's version: *I'll tell you what I believe if you tell me who else believes it.*

Malcolm Gladwell pointed out the absurdity of her position by tweeting, "I signed the Harpers letter because there were lots of people who also signed the Harpers letter whose views I disagreed with. I thought that was the point of the Harpers letter."

Boylan's having so publicly distanced herself from the letter put her in a bit of a pickle when Rushdie was attacked. How to get in on the action without alluding to her own abandonment of him? She found a way, retweeting the announcement of a PEN event to be held in solidarity with the writer: PEN members would read from his work at an event held on the steps of the Metropolitan Museum of Art. Above the announcement, she wrote, with apparently zero self-reflection, "Show Up for Salman."

I did not see her name on the list of writers who were to read from his work at the event, but the announcement said the list was "still in formation." Boylan often comes to New York for PEN events, and I did wonder if she might go and read from his work; that would have been courageous, and it would certainly cancel out her earlier action.

But this suspenseful interlude was cut short the day before the event, when she tweeted, "I'm off to my cousin's house in Ireland tomorrow."

After a few days in the country, she tweeted—in the spirit of merriment, but not, apparently, of self-knowledge—"'Boylan,' btw, in Irish, means 'oath breaker' or 'liar.'"

THE CONCEPT OF FREE SPEECH evolved in the West for 2,000 years, beginning with the Athenians (although not without a few setbacks, such as the death of Socrates). But America was the first country in history to enshrine a formal, legal, and enforceable protection for free expression, ensuring that people have the right to speak no matter who's pissed off or how powerful they are.

A

Whenever a society collapses in on itself, free speech is the first thing to go. That's how you know we're in the process of closing up shop. Our legal protections remain in place—that's why so many of us were able to smack the Trump piñata to such effect—but the *culture* of free speech is eroding every day. Ask an Oberlin student—fresh outta Shaker Heights, coming in hot, with a heart as big as all outdoors and a 3 in AP Bio—to tell you what speech is acceptable, and she'll tell you that it's speech that doesn't hurt the feelings of anyone belonging to a protected class.

And here we are, running out the clock on the American epilogue. The people on the far right are dangerous lunatics and millions on even the center left want to rewrite the genetic code.

If you don't want to stick around for the fire sale (*The Federalist Papers*! "Letter From Birmingham Jail"! Everything must go!) and you're not too eager to get knifed on a Friday morning because of something you said, you might want to look into relocating to one of the other countries shaped by the principles of the American Revolution. They aren't hard to find. Just go to Google and type in *the free world*.

THE DARK POWER OF
FRATERNITIES

March 2014

ONE WARM SPRING NIGHT IN 2011, a young man named Travis Hughes stood on the back deck of the Alpha Tau Omega fraternity house at Marshall University, in West Virginia, and was struck by what seemed to him—under the influence of powerful inebriants, not least among them the clear ether of youth itself—to be an excellent idea: He would shove a bottle rocket up his ass and blast it into the sweet night air. And perhaps it *was* an excellent idea. What was not an excellent idea, however, was to misjudge the relative tightness of a 20-year-old sphincter and the propulsive reliability of a 20-cent bottle rocket. What followed ignition was not the bright report of a successful blastoff, but the muffled thud of fire in the hole.

Also on the deck, and also in the thrall of the night's pleasures, was one Louis Helmburg III, an education major and ace benchwarmer for the Thundering Herd baseball team. His response to the proposed launch was the obvious one: He reportedly whipped out his cellphone to record it on video, which would turn out to be yet another of the night's seemingly excellent but ultimately misguided ideas. When the bottle rocket exploded in Hughes's rectum, Helmburg was seized by the kind of battlefield panic that has claimed brave men from outfits far more illustrious than even the Thundering Herd. Terrified, he staggered away from the human bomb and fell off the deck.

Fortunately for him, and adding to the Chaplinesque aspect of the night's miseries, the deck was no more than four feet off the ground, but such was the urgency of his escape that he managed to get himself wedged between the structure and an air-conditioning unit, sustaining injuries that would require medical attention, cut short his baseball season, and—in the fullness of time—pit him against the mighty forces of the Alpha Tau Omega national organization, which had been waiting for him.

It takes a certain kind of personal-injury lawyer to look at the facts of this glittering night and wrest from them a plausible plaintiff and defendant, unless it were possible for Travis Hughes to be sued by his own anus. But the fraternity lawsuit is a lucrative mini-segment of the personal-injury business, and if ever there was a deck that ought to have had a railing, it was the one that served as a nighttime think tank and party-idea testing ground for the brain trust of the Theta Omicron Chapter of Alpha Tau Omega and its honored guests—including these two knuckleheads, who didn't even belong to the frater- nity. Moreover, the building codes of Huntington, West

Virginia, are unambiguous on the necessity of railings on elevated decks. Whether Helmburg stumbled in reaction to an exploding party guest or to the Second Coming of Jesus Christ is immaterial; there should have been a railing to catch him.

And so it was that Louis Helmburg III joined forces with Timothy P. Rosinsky, Esq., a slip-and-fall lawyer from Huntington who had experience also with dog-bite, DUI, car-repossession, and drug cases. The events of that night, laid out in Helmburg's complaint, suggested a relatively straightforward lawsuit. But the suit would turn out to have its own repeated failures to launch and unintended collateral damage, and it would include an ever-widening and desperate search for potential defendants willing to foot the modest bill for Helmburg's documented injuries. Sending a lawyer without special expertise in wrangling with fraternities to sue one of them is like sending a Boy Scout to sort out the unpleasantness in Afghanistan. Who knows? The kid could get lucky. But it never hurts—preparedness and all that—to send him off with a body bag.

College fraternities—by which term of art I refer to the formerly all-white, now nominally integrated men's "general" or "social" fraternities, and not the several other types of fraternities on American campuses (religious, ethnic, academic)—are as old, almost, as the republic. In a sense, they are older: They emanated in part from the

A

Freemasons, of which George Washington himself was a member. When arguments are made in their favor, they are arguments in defense of a foundational experience for millions of American young men, and of a system that helped build American higher education as we know it. Fraternities also provide their members with matchless leadership training. While the system has produced its share of poets, aesthetes, and Henry James scholars, it is far more famous for its success in the powerhouse fraternity fields of business, law, and politics. An astonishing number of CEOs of *Fortune* 500 companies, congressmen and male senators, and American presidents have belonged to fraternities. Many more thousands of American men count their fraternal experience—and the friendships made within it—as among the most valuable in their lives. The organizations raise millions of dollars for worthy causes, contribute millions of hours in community service, and seek to steer young men toward lives of service and honorable action. They also have a long, dark history of violence against their own members and visitors to their houses, which makes them in many respects at odds with the core mission of college itself.

Lawsuits against fraternities are becoming a growing matter of public interest, in part because they record such lurid events, some of them ludicrous, many more of them horrendous. For every butt bomb, there's a complaint of manslaughter, rape, sexual torture, psychological trauma.

A recent series of articles on fraternities by Bloomberg News's David Glovin and John Hechinger notes that since 2005, more than 60 people—the majority of them students—have died in incidents linked to fraternities, a sobering number in itself, but one that is dwarfed by the numbers of serious injuries, assaults, and sexual crimes that regularly take place in these houses. Many people believe that violent hazing is the most dangerous event associated with fraternity life, but hazing causes a relatively small percentage of these injuries. Because of a variety of forces, all this harm—and the behaviors that lead to it—has lately been moving out of the shadows of private disciplinary hearings and silent suffering, and into the bright light of civil lawsuits, giving us a clear picture of some of the more forbidding truths about fraternity life. While many of these suits never make it to trial, disappearing into confidential settlements (as did that of Louis Helmburg III, nearly two years after he filed his lawsuit) or melting away once plaintiffs recognize the powerful and monolithic forces they are up against, the narratives they leave behind in their complaints—all of them matters of public record—comprise a rich and potent testimony to the kinds of experiences regularly taking place on college campuses. Tellingly, the material facts of these complaints are rarely in dispute; what is contested, most often, is only liability.

A

Far from being freakish and unpredictable events, fatal and near-fatal falls from fraternity-house roofs, balconies, windows, and sleeping porches are fairly regular occurrences across the country.

I have spent most of the past year looking deeply into the questions posed by these lawsuits, and more generally into the particular nature of fraternity life on the modern American campus. Much of what I found challenged my beliefs about the system, assumptions that I came to see as grossly outdated, not because the nature of fraternity life has changed so much, but rather because life at the contemporary university has gone through such a profound transformation in the past quarter century. I found that the ways in which the system exerts its power—and maintains its longevity—in the face of the many potentially antagonistic priorities in contemporary higher education commanded my grudging respect. Fraternity tradition at its most essential is rooted in a set of old, deeply American, morally unassailable convictions, some of which—such as a young man's right to the freedom of association—emanate from the Constitution itself. In contrast, much of the policy governing college campuses today is rooted in the loose soil of a set of political and social fashions that change with the season, and that tend not to hold up to any kind of penetrating challenge. And this is why—to answer the vexing question "why don't colleges just get rid of their bad fraternities?"—the system, and its individual frats, have only grown in power and influence. Indeed, in many substantive ways, fraternities are now mightier than the colleges and universities that host them.

THE ENTIRE MULTIBILLION-DOLLAR, 2,000-campus American college system—with its armies of salaried professors, administrators, librarians, bursars, secretaries, admissions officers, alumni liaisons, development-office workers, coaches, groundskeepers, janitors, maintenance workers, psychologists, nurses, trainers, technology-support staffers, residence-life personnel, cafeteria workers, diversity-compliance officers, the whole shebang—depends overwhelmingly for its very existence on one resource: an ever-renewing supply of fee-paying undergraduates. It could never attract hundreds of thousands of them each year—many of them woefully unprepared for the experience, a staggering number (some 40 percent) destined never to get a degree, more than 60 percent of them saddled with student loans that they very well may carry with them to their deathbeds—if the experience were not accurately marketed as a blast. They show up on campus lugging enormous Bed Bath & Beyond bags crammed with "essentials," and with new laptop computers, on which they will surf Facebook and Tumblr while some coot down at the lectern bangs on about Maslow's hierarchy and tries to make his PowerPoint slides appear

A

right side up. Many of these consumer goods have been purchased with money from the very student loans that will haunt them for so long, but no matter: It's college; any cost can be justified. The kids arrive eager to hurl themselves upon the pasta bars and the climbing walls, to splash into the 12-person Jacuzzis and lounge around the outdoor fire pits, all of which have been constructed in a blatant effort to woo them away from competitors. They swipe prepaid cards in dormitory vending machines to acquire whatever tanning wipes or earbuds or condoms or lube or energy drinks the occasion seems to require. And every moment of the experience is sweetened by the general understanding that with each kegger and rager, each lazy afternoon spent snoozing on the quad (a forgotten highlighter slowly drying out on the open pages of *Introduction to Economics*, a Coke Zero sweating beside it), they are actively engaged in the most significant act of self-improvement available to an American young person: college!

That all of this fun is somehow as essential as the education itself—is somehow part of a benevolent and ultimately edifying process of "growing up"—is one of the main reasons so many parents who are themselves in rocky financial shape will make economically ruinous decisions to support a four-year-residential-college experience for their children. There are many thousands of American undergraduates whose economic futures (and those of their parents) would be far brighter if they knocked off some of their general-education requirements online, or at the local community college—for pennies on the dollar—before entering the Weimar Republic of traditional-college pricing. But college education, like weddings and funerals, tends to prompt irrational financial decision making, and so here we are. Add another pesto flavor to the pasta bar, Dean Roland! We just lost another kid to online ed!

That pursuing a bachelor's degree might be something other than a deeply ascetic and generally miserable experience was once a preposterous idea. American colleges came into being with the express purpose of training young men for the ministry, a preparation that was marked by a chilly round of early risings, Greek and Latin recitations, religious study, and strict discipline meted out by a dour faculty—along with expectations of both temperance and chastity. Hardly conditions that would augur the current trillion-dollar student-loan balloon that hovers over us like a preignition *Hindenburg*. But sexual frustration and homiletics would not last forever as the hallmarks of American college life.

In 1825, at Union College, in upstate New York (hardly a garden of earthly delights in the best of circumstances, but surely a gulag experience for those stuck at Union; imagine studying Thessalonians in the ass-cracking cold of a Schenectady February), a small group of young men came up with a creative act of rebellion against the fun-busters who had them down: the formation of a secret club, which they grandly named the Kappa Alpha Society. Word of the group spread, and a new kind of college institution was founded, and with it a brand-new notion: that going to college could include some pleasure. It was the American age of societies, and this new type fit right in. As Nicholas L. Syrett observes in his excellent history of white men's college fraternities, *The Company He Keeps*, these early fraternities were in every way a measure of their time. They combined the secret handshakes and passwords of small boys' clubs; the symbols and rituals of Freemasonry; the new national interest in Greek, as opposed to Roman, culture as a model for an emerging citizenry; and the popularity of literary societies, elements of which—oratory, recitation, and the presentation of essays—the early fraternities included. Fraternities also gave young college men a way of behaving and of thinking about themselves that quickly took on surprisingly modern dimensions.

From the very beginning, fraternities were loathed by the grown-ups running colleges, who tried to banish them. But independence from overbearing faculties—existing on a plane beyond the reach of discipline—was, in large measure, the point of fraternity membership; far from fearing the opprobrium of their knock-kneed overlords, the young men relished and even courted it. When colleges tried to shut them down, fraternities asserted that any threat to men's membership in the clubs constituted an infringement of their right to freedom of association. It was, at best, a legally delicate argument, but it was a symbolically potent one, and it has withstood through the years. The powerful and well-funded political-action committee that represents fraternities in Washington has fought successfully to ensure that freedom-of-association language is included in all higher-education reauthorization legislation, thus "disallowing public Universities the ability to ban fraternities."

Perhaps the best testament to the deep power of fraternities is how quickly and widely they spread. Soon after Gold Rush money began flowing into the newly established state of California—giving rise to the improbable idea of building a great American university on the shores of the Pacific Ocean—fraternity men staked their own claim: A campus in Berkeley had existed barely a year before the brothers of Phi Delta Theta arrived to initiate new members. The thing to remember about fraternities is that when Kappa Alpha was founded at Union, in all of the United States there were only 4,600 college students; fraternities exist as deeply in the groundwater of American higher education as religious study—and have retained a far greater presence in the lives of modern students.

In fairly short order, a paradox began to emerge, one that exists to this day. While the fraternities continued to

A

exert their independence from the colleges with which they were affiliated, these same colleges started to develop an increasingly bedeviling kind of interdependence with the accursed societies. To begin with, the fraternities involved themselves very deeply in the business of student housing, which provided tremendous financial savings to their host institutions, and allowed them to expand the number of students they could admit. Today, one in eight American students at four-year colleges lives in a Greek house, and a conservative estimate of the collective value of these houses across the country is $3 billion. Greek housing constitutes a troubling fact for college administrators (the majority of fraternity-related deaths occur in and around fraternity houses, over which the schools have limited and widely varying levels of operational oversight) and also a great boon to them (saving them untold millions of dollars in the construction and maintenance of campus-owned and -controlled dormitories).

Moreover, fraternities tie alumni to their colleges in a powerful and lucrative way. At least one study has affirmed what had long been assumed: that fraternity men tend to be generous to their alma maters. Furthermore, fraternities provide colleges with unlimited social programming of a kind that is highly attractive to legions of potential students, most of whom are not applying to ivy-covered rejection factories, but rather to vast public institutions and obscure private colleges that are desperate for students. When Mom is trying—against all better judgment—to persuade lackluster Joe Jr. to go to college, she gets a huge assist when she drives him over to State and he gets an eyeful of frat row. Joe Jr. may be slow to grasp even the most elemental concepts of math and English (his first two years of expensive college study will largely be spent in remediation of the subjects he should have learned, for free, in high school), but one look at the Fiji house and he gets the message: Kids are getting laid here; kids are having fun. Maybe he ought to snuff out the joint and take a second look at that application Mom keeps pushing across the kitchen table.

Will he be in increased physical jeopardy if he joins one of these clubs? The fraternity industry says no. When confronted with evidence of student injury and death in their houses, fraternities claim they are no worse than any other campus group; that they have become "target defendants," prey to the avarice of tort lawyers excited by their many assets and extensive liability coverage. It is true that fraternity lawsuits tend to involve at least one, and often more, of the four horsemen of the student-life apocalypse, a set of factors that exist far beyond frat row and that are currently bringing college presidents to their knees. First and foremost of these is the binge-drinking epidemic, which anyone outside the problem has a hard time grasping as serious (everyone drinks in college!) and which anyone with knowledge of the current situation understands

A

as a lurid and complicated disaster. The second is the issue of sexual assault of female undergraduates by their male peers, a subject of urgent importance but one that remains stubbornly difficult even to quantify, let alone rectify, although it absorbs huge amounts of student interest, outrage, institutional funding, and—increasingly—federal attention. The third is the growing pervasiveness of violent hazing on campus, an art form that reaches its apogee at fraternities, but that has lately spread to all sorts of student groups. And the fourth is the fact that Boomers, who in their own days destroyed the doctrine of *in loco parentis* so that they could party in blissful, unsupervised freedom, have grown up into the helicopter parents of today, holding fiercely to a pair of mutually exclusive desires: on the one hand that their kids get to experience the same unfettered personal freedoms of college that they remember so fondly, and on the other that the colleges work hard to protect the physical and emotional well-being of their precious children.

But it's impossible to examine particular types of campus calamity and not find that a large number of them cluster at fraternity houses. Surely they have cornered the market in injuries to the buttocks. The number of lawsuits that involve paddling gone wrong, or branding that necessitated skin grafts, or a particular variety of sexual torture reserved for hazing and best not described in the gentle pages of *The Atlantic*, is astounding. To say nothing of the

University of Tennessee frat boy who got dropped off, insensate, at the university hospital's emergency room and was originally assumed to be the victim of a sexual assault, and only later turned out to have damaged his rectum by allegedly pumping wine into it through an enema hose, as had his pals.

Or, to turn away from the buttocks, as surely a good number of fraternity men would be well advised to do, consider another type of fraternity injury: the tendency of brothers and their guests to get liquored up and fall off—or out of—the damn houses is a story in itself.

THE CAMPUSES OF WASHINGTON State University and the University of Idaho are located some eight miles apart in the vast agricultural region of the Northwest known as the Palouse. It was at the latter institution that the 19-year-old sophomore and newly minted Delta Delta Delta pledge Amanda Andaverde arrived in August of 2009, although she had scarcely moved into the Tri Delta house and registered for classes before she was at the center of events that would leave her with brain damage and cast her as the plaintiff in a major lawsuit filed on her behalf by her devastated parents.

It would have been an unremarkable Wednesday evening—focused on the kind of partying and hooking up that are frequent pleasures of modern sorority women—save for its hideous end. Andaverde and her sorority sisters

A

began the night at Sigma Chi, where the "sorority ladies" drank alcohol and spent the evening with "dates" they had been assigned during a party game. (The language of Andaverde's legal complaint often seems couched in a combination of '50s lingo and polite euphemism, intended perhaps to preclude a conservative Idaho jury from making moralistic judgments about the plaintiff's behavior.) The charms of Andaverde's assigned date ran thin, apparently, because close to midnight, she left him and made her way over to the Sigma Alpha Epsilon house, where she quickly ended up on the third-floor sleeping porch.

Many fraternity houses, especially older ones, have sleeping porches—sometimes called "cold airs" or "rack rooms"—typically located on the top floor of the buildings' gable ends. They are large rooms filled with bunks, some of which are stacked in triple tiers, and their large windows are often left open, even in the coldest months. Many fraternity members have exceedingly fond memories of their time on the porches, which they view—like so many fraternity traditions—as a simultaneously vexing and bonding experience. Although these group sleeping arrangements were once considered an impediment to a young man's sex life, the hookup culture, in which privacy is no longer a requirement of sexual activity, has changed that, and the sleeping-porch experience is once again coming into favor. For a variety of reasons, sleeping porches feature in a number of lawsuits, pointing to an astonishing fact: Despite fraternity houses' position as de facto residence halls for so many American college students, safety features are decidedly spotty; about half of them don't even have fire sprinklers.

According to the complaint, shortly after arriving at SAE, Andaverde ran into a friend of hers, and he took her up to the sleeping porch, where he introduced her to a pal of his named Joseph Cody Cook. Andaverde and Cook talked, then climbed into Cook's bunk, where the two began kissing. It is at this point that the language of the suit finally frees itself of euphemism and reveals the fearsome power of the unambiguous, declarative sentence: "Amanda rolled onto her shoulder toward the exterior wall, and suddenly, quickly, and unexpectedly dropped off Cook's mattress into the open exterior window, falling from the third-floor 'sleeping porch' to the cement approximately 25 feet below."

The injuries were devastating and included permanent brain injury. Andaverde was airlifted to a trauma center in Seattle, where she remained for many weeks; in the early days of her care, it seemed she might not survive. Eventually, however, she improved enough to leave the hospital and was transferred to a series of rehabilitation centers, where she spent many months learning to regain basic functions. Police, interviewed about the case, defended themselves the way police departments in college towns all over the country reasonably defend themselves

A

when accused of not preventing a fraternity-house disaster: "We just can't send undercover people into private houses or private parties," said David Duke, the Moscow, Idaho, assistant chief of police.

Local news outlets covered Andaverde's plight widely and sympathetically, although the optimism with which her "miraculous" recovery was celebrated was perhaps exaggerated. A television news report dedicated to that miracle revealed a young woman who, while she had escaped death, had clearly been grievously injured. As the reporter interviewed her mother, Andaverde sat in a wheelchair. When her hands were not propped on a black lap tray latched to the chair, she struggled to grasp a crayon and run it across the pages of a children's coloring book, or to place the six large pieces of a simple puzzle—square, triangle, circle—into their spaces. She eventually improved from this desperate state—learning to walk and dress herself—but she was a far cry from the student of veterinary medicine she had once been.

The local inclinations to see a badly injured college student as a figure deserving of community support, and to view even a limited recovery as evidence of the goodness of God, are not unaligned with regional preferences for self-reliance and for taking responsibility for one's own actions, however dire the consequences. The inevitable court case—in which the Andaverde family named not only SAE and Tri Delta as defendants, but also the

University of Idaho and the Idaho State Board of Education—was dismissed on summary judgment because there was no dispute that Andaverde fell out of an open window, and because there was no evidence of an inherently dangerous condition in the house: That the window was open was obvious to anyone who walked into the room. The court determined that no other person or institution had a duty to protect Amanda from the actions and decisions—the decision to drink alcohol, as a minor; the decision to climb into a bunk bed; the impulse to roll over—that led to her accident.

Andaverde's case seemed to me to be an isolated tragedy, until I sent away to the Latah County courthouse for a copy of the complaint and discovered within it this sentence: "Amanda's fall was the second fall of a student from an upper-story fraternity house window at the University of Idaho within approximately a two-week period." This struck me as an astonishing coincidence. I looked into the matter and found that, indeed, a 20-year-old man named Shane Meyer had fallen from the third-floor window of the Delta Tau Delta house just 12 days before Andaverde's fall from SAE; not surprisingly, the police reported that "alcohol may have been a factor." He, too, had been airlifted to Seattle, and incredibly, the two fought for their lives in the same critical-care unit at Harborview Medical Center. I became intrigued by this kind of injury and began to do some more checking into the subject. I

A

discovered that two months *after* Andaverde's fall, a 20-year-old student at Washington State—"quite intoxicated," in the laconic assessment of a local cop—pitched forward and fell from a third-floor window of Alpha Kappa Lambda, escaping serious injury when his fall was broken by an SUV parked below. That these three events were not greeted on either campus by any kind of clamoring sense of urgency—that they were, rather, met with a resigned sort of "here we go again" attitude by campus administrators and with what appeared to be the pro forma appointment of an investigative task force—sparked my interest, and so it was that I entered the bizarre world of falls from fraternity houses, which, far from being freakish and unpredictable events, are in fact fairly regular occurrences across the country.

During the 2012–13 school year on the Palouse—where students from the two campuses often share apartments and attend parties at each other's schools—the falls continued. In September, a student suffered serious injuries after falling off the roof of the Alpha Tau Omega house at the University of Idaho, and two days later a Washington State student fell three stories from a window at Phi Kappa Tau. In November, a 19-year-old suffered critical head injuries when he fell backward off a second-floor balcony at the Washington State Lambda Chi Alpha house, necessitating the surgical removal of part of his skull. In April, a University of Idaho student named

Krysta Huft filed a suit against the Delta Chi fraternity, seeking damages for a broken pelvis resulting from a 2011 fall, which she claims was from the house's third-story sleeping porch onto a basketball court beneath it.

I decided to widen my search, and quickly discovered that this is not a phenomenon particular to the Northwest. Across the country, kids fall—disastrously—from the upper heights of fraternity houses with some regularity. They tumble from the open windows they are trying to urinate out of, slip off roofs, lose their grasp on drainpipes, misjudge the width of fire-escape landings. On February 25, 2012, a student at the University of California at Berkeley attempted to climb down the drainpipe of the Phi Gamma Delta house, fell, and suffered devastating injuries; on April 14 of the same year, a 21-year-old student at Gannon University, in Pennsylvania, died after a fall from the second-floor balcony of the Alpha Phi Delta house the night before; on May 13, a Cornell student was airlifted to a trauma center after falling from the fire escape at Delta Chi; on October 13, a student at James Madison University fell from the roof of the three-story Delta Chi house and was airlifted to the University of Virginia hospital; on December 1, a 19-year-old woman fell eight feet from the Sigma Alpha Mu house at Penn State.

This summer brought little relief. On July 13, a man fell more than 30 feet from a third-story window at the Theta Delta Chi house at the University of Washington and was transported to Harborview Medical Center (which must by now be developing a subspecialty in such injuries); that same day, a Dartmouth College employee, apparently having consumed LSD and marijuana, fell out of a second-story window of the Sigma Nu house and was seriously injured. On August 13, a student at the University of Oklahoma fell face-first off a balcony of the SAE house; the next day, a woman fell from a second-story fire escape at Phi Kappa Tau at Washington State University.

The current school year began, and still the falls continued. In September, a student at Washington State fell down a flight of stairs in the Delta Chi house and was rendered unconscious; a University of Minnesota student was hospitalized after falling off a second-floor balcony of the Phi Kappa Psi house; a Northwestern student was listed in critical condition after falling out of a third-floor window of the Phi Gamma Delta house; and an MIT student injured his head and genitals after falling through a skylight at the Phi Sigma Kappa house and landing some 40 feet below.

These falls, of course, are in addition to the many other kinds of havoc and tragedy associated with fraternities. On the Palouse, such incidents include the January 2013 death of 18-year-old Joseph Wiederrick, a University of Idaho freshman who had made the dean's list his first semester, and who had plans to become an architect. He had attended a party at SAE (of which he was not a member) and then wandered, apparently drunk and lost, for five miles before freezing to death under a bridge. They also include the March 2013 conviction of Jesse M. Vierstra, who, while visiting Sigma Chi over the University of Idaho's homecoming weekend, raped an 18-year-old freshman in the bushes outside the house. (He is appealing the decision.)

The notion that fraternities are target defendants did not hold true in my investigation. College students can (and do) fall out of just about any kind of residence, of course. But during the period of time under consideration, serious falls from fraternity houses on the two Palouse campuses far outnumbered those from other types of student residences, including privately owned apartments occupied by students. I began to view Amanda Andaverde's situation in a new light. Why are so many colleges allowing students to live and party in such unsafe locations? And why do the lawsuits against fraternities for this kind of serious injury and death—so predictable and so preventable—have such a hard time getting traction? The answers lie in the recent history of fraternities and the colleges and universities that host them.

WHAT ALL OF THESE LAWSUITS ultimately concern is a crucially important question in higher education, one that legal scholars have been grappling with for the past half century. This question is perhaps most elegantly expressed in the subtitle of Robert D. Bickel and Peter F. Lake's authoritative 1999 book on the subject, *The Rights and Responsibilities of the Modern University: Who Assumes the Risks of College Life?*

The answer to this question has been steadily evolving ever since the 1960s, when dramatic changes took place on American campuses, changes that affected both a university's ability to control student behavior and the status of fraternities in the undergraduate firmament. During this period of student unrest, the fraternities—long the unquestioned leaders in the area of sabotaging or ignoring the patriarchal control of school administrators—became the exact opposite: representatives of the very status quo the new activists sought to overthrow. Suddenly their beer bashes and sorority mixers, their panty raids and obsession with the big game, seemed impossibly reactionary when compared with the mind-altering drugs being sampled in off-campus apartments where sexual liberation was being born and the Little Red Book proved, if nothing else, a fantastic coaster for a leaky bong.

American students sought to wrest themselves entirely from the disciplinary control of their colleges and universities, institutions that had historically operated *in loco parentis*, carefully monitoring the private behavior of undergraduates. The students of the new era wanted nothing to do with that infantilizing way of existence, and fought to rid themselves of the various curfews, dorm mothers, demerit systems, and other modes of institutional oppression. If they were old enough to die in Vietnam, powerful enough to overthrow a president, groovy enough to expand their minds with LSD and free love, then they certainly didn't need their own colleges—the very places where they were forming their radical, nation-changing ideas—to treat them like teenyboppers in need of a sock hop and a chaperone. It was a turning point: American colleges began to regard their students not as dependents whose private lives they must shape and monitor, but as adult consumers whose contract was solely for an education, not an upbringing. The doctrine of *in loco parentis* was abolished at school after school. Through it all, fraternities—for so long the repositories of the most outrageous behavior—moldered, all but forgotten. Membership fell sharply, fraternity houses slid into increasing states of disrepair, and hundreds of chapters closed.

ANIMAL HOUSE, RELEASED IN 1978, at once predicted and to no small extent occasioned the roaring return of fraternity life that began in the early '80s and that gave birth to today's vital Greek scene. The casting of John Belushi was essential to the movie's influence: No one had greater credibility in the post-'60s youth culture. If something as fundamentally reactionary as fraternity membership was going to replace something as fundamentally radical as student unrest, it would need to align itself with someone whose bona fides among young, white, middle-class males were unassailable. In this newly forming culture, the drugs and personal liberation of the '60s would be paired with the self-serving materialism of the '80s, all of which made partying for its own sake—and not as a philosophical adjunct to solving some complicated problem in Southeast Asia—a righteous activity for the pampered young collegian. Fraternity life was reborn with a vengeance.

It was an entirely new kind of student who arrived at the doors of those great and crumbling mansions: at once deeply attracted to the ceremony and formality of fraternity life and yet utterly transformed by the social revolutions of the past decades. These new members and their countless guests brought with them hard drugs, new and ever-developing sexual attitudes, and a stunningly high tolerance for squalor (never had middle- and upper-middle-class American young people lived in such filth as did '60s and '70s college kids who were intent on rejecting their parents' bourgeois ways). Furthermore, in 1984 Congress passed the National Minimum Drinking Age Act, with the ultimate result of raising the legal drinking age to 21 in all 50 states. This change moved college partying away from bars and college-sponsored events and toward private houses—an ideal situation for fraternities. When these advances were combined with the evergreen fraternity traditions of violent hazing and brawling among rival frats, the scene quickly became wildly dangerous.

Adult supervision was nowhere to be found. Colleges had little authority to intervene in what took place in the personal lives of its students visiting private property. Fraternities, eager to provide their members with the independence that is at the heart of the system—and responsive to members' wishes for the same level of freedom that non-Greek students enjoyed—had largely gotten rid of the live-in resident advisers who had once provided some sort of check on the brothers. With these conditions in place, lawsuits began to pour in.

No sooner has a national fraternity rolled out a new "Men of Principle" or "True Gentlemen" campaign than reports of a lurid disaster in some prominent or far-flung chapter undermine the whole thing.

The mid-1980s were a treacherous time to be the defendant in a tort lawsuit. Personal-injury cases had undergone a long shift to the plaintiff's advantage; the theory of comparative negligence—by which an individual can acknowledge his or her own partial responsibility for an injury yet still recover damages from a defendant— had become the standard; the era of huge jury verdicts was at hand. Americans in vast numbers—motivated perhaps in part by the possibility of financial recompense, and in part by a new national impetus to move personal suffering from the sphere of private sorrow to that of public

A

confession and complaint—began to sue those who had damaged them. Many fraternity lawsuits listed the relevant college or university among the defendants, a practice still common among less experienced plaintiff's attorneys. These institutions possess deep reservoirs of liability coverage, but students rarely recover significant funds from their schools. As Amanda Andaverde's attorneys discovered the hard way, a great deal of time and money can be spent seeking damages from institutions of higher learning, which can be protected by everything from sovereign immunity and damage caps (in the case of public universities), to their limited ability to monitor the private behavior of their students. But for the fraternities themselves, it was a far different story.

So recently and robustly brought back to life, the fraternities now faced the most serious threat to their existence they had ever experienced. A single lawsuit had the potential to devastate a fraternity. In 1985, a young man grievously injured in a Kappa Alpha–related accident reached a settlement with the fraternity that, over the course of his lifetime, could amount to some $21 million—a sum that caught the attention of everyone in the Greek world. Liability insurance became both ruinously expensive and increasingly difficult to obtain. The insurance industry ranked American fraternities as the sixth-worst insurance risk in the country—just ahead of toxic-waste-removal companies. "You guys are nuts," an insurance representative told a fraternity CEO in 1989, just before canceling the organization's coverage; "you can't operate like this much longer."

For fraternities to survive, they needed to do four separate but related things: Take the task of acquiring insurance out of the hands of the local chapters and place it in the hands of the vast national organizations; develop procedures and policies that would transfer as much of their liability as possible to outside parties; find new and creative means of protecting their massive assets from juries; and—perhaps most important of all—find a way of indemnifying the national and local organizations from the dangerous and illegal behavior of some of their undergraduate members. The way fraternities accomplished all of this is the underlying story in the lawsuits they face, and it is something that few members—and, I would wager, even fewer parents of members—grasp completely, comprising a set of realities you should absolutely understand in detail if your son ever decides to join a fraternity.

SELF-INSURANCE WAS AN OBVIOUS MEANS for combating prohibitive insurance pricing and the widening reluctance to insure fraternities. In 1992, four fraternities created what was first called the Fraternity Risk Management Trust, a vast sum of money used for reinsurance. Today, 32 fraternities belong to this trust. In 2006, a group of seven other fraternities bought their own insurance

A

broker, James R. Favor, which now insures many others. More important than self-insurance, however, was the development of a risk-management policy that would become—across these huge national outfits and their hundreds of individual chapters—the industry standard. This was accomplished by the creation of something called the Fraternal Information and Programming Group (FIPG), which in the mid-1980s developed a comprehensive risk-management policy for fraternities that is regularly updated. Currently 32 fraternities are members of the FIPG and adhere to this policy, or to their own even more rigorous versions. One fraternity expert told me that even non-FIPG frats have similar policies, many based in large measure on FIPG's, which is seen as something of a blueprint. In a certain sense, you may *think* you belong to Tau Kappa Epsilon or Sigma Nu or Delta Tau Delta—but if you find yourself a part of life-changing litigation involving one of those outfits, what you really belong to is FIPG, because its risk-management policy (and your adherence to or violation of it) will determine your fate far more than the vows you made during your initiation ritual—vows composed by long-dead men who had never even heard of the concept of fraternity insurance.

FIPG regularly produces a risk-management manual—the current version is 50 pages—that lays out a wide range of (optional) best practices. If the manual were *Anna Karenina*, alcohol policy would be its farming reform: the buzz-killing subplot that quickly reveals itself to be an authorial obsession. For good reason: The majority of all fraternity insurance claims involve booze—I have read hundreds of fraternity incident reports, not one of which describes an event where massive amounts of alcohol weren't part of the problem—and the need to manage or transfer risk presented by alcohol is perhaps the most important factor in protecting the system's longevity. Any plaintiff's attorney worth his salt knows how to use relevant social-host and dramshop laws against a fraternity; to avoid this kind of liability, the fraternity needs to establish that the young men being charged were not acting within the scope of their status as fraternity members. Once they violated their frat's alcohol policy, they parted company with the frat. It's a neat piece of logic: The very fact that a young man finds himself in need of insurance coverage is often grounds for denying it to him.

So: alcohol and the fraternity man. Despite everything you may think you know about life on frat row, there are actually only two FIPG-approved means of serving drinks at a frat party. The first is to hire a third-party vendor who will sell drinks and to whom some liability—most significant, that of checking whether drinkers are of legal age—will be transferred. The second and far more common is to have a BYO event, in which the liability for each bottle of alcohol resides solely in the person who brought it. If you think this is in any way a casual system, then you have never read either the FIPG risk-management manual or its sister publication, an essay written in the surrealist vein titled "Making Bring Your Own Beverage Events Happen."

THE OFFICIAL BYO SYSTEM is like something dreamed up by a committee of Soviet bureaucrats and Irish nuns. It begins with the composition— no fewer than 24 hours before the party—of a comprehensive guest list. This guest list does not serve the happy function of ensuring a perfect mix of types and temperaments at the festivity; rather, it limits attendance—and ensures that the frat is in possession of "a witness list in the event something does occur which may end up in court two or more years later." Provided a fraternity member—let's call him Larry—is older than 21 (which the great majority of members, like the great majority of all college students, are not), he is allowed to bring six (and no more) beers *or* four (and no more) wine coolers to the party. (FIPG's admiration for the wine-cooler four-pack suggests that at least some aspects of the foundational document—including its recommendation for throwing a *M*A*S*H*-themed party as recently as 2007—have not received much of an overhaul since its first edition, published in the mid-'80s.) OK, so Larry brings a six-pack. The first stop, depending on which fraternity he belongs to: a "sober check point," at which he is subjected to an examination. Does he appear to have already consumed any alcohol? Is he in any way "known" to have done so? If he passes, he hands over his ID for inspection. Next he must do business with a "sober monitor." This person relieves him of the six-pack, hands him a ticket indicating the precise type of beer he brought, and ideally affixes a "non breakable except by cutting" wristband to his person; only then can Larry retrieve his beers, one at a time, for his own personal consumption. If any are left over at the end of the party, his fraternity will secure them until the next day, when Larry can be reunited with his unconsumed beers, unless his frat decided to "eliminate" them overnight. Weaknesses in the system include the fact that all of these people coming between Larry and his beer—the sober monitors and ID checkers and militarized barkeeps—are Larry's fraternity brothers, who are among his closest buddies and who have pledged him lifelong fealty during candlelit ceremonies rife with Masonic mumbo jumbo and the fluttering language of 19th-century romantic friendship. Note also that these policies make it possible for fraternities to be the one industry in the country in which every aspect of serving alcohol can be monitored and managed by people who are legally too young to drink it.

Clearly, a great number of fraternity members will, at some point in their undergraduate career, violate their frat's alcohol policy regarding the six beers—and just as clearly, the great majority will never face any legal consequences for doing so. But when the inevitable catastrophes do happen, that policy can come to seem more like a cynical hoax than a real-world solution to a serious problem. When something terrible takes place—a young man plummets from a roof, a young woman is assaulted, a fraternity brother is subjected to the kind of sexual sadism that appears all too often in fraternity lawsuits—any small violation of policy can leave fraternity members twisting in the wind. Consider the following scenario: Larry makes a small, human-size mistake one night. Instead of waiting for the slow drip of six warm beers, he brings a bottle of Maker's Mark to the party, and—in the spirit of not being a weirdo or a dick—he shares it, at one point pouring a couple of ounces into the passing Solo cup of a kid who's running on empty and asks him for a shot. Larry never sees the kid again that night—not many people do; he ends up drinking himself to death in an upstairs bedroom. In the sad fullness of time, the night's horror is turned into a lawsuit, in which Larry becomes a named defendant. Thanks in part to the guest/witness list, Larry can be cut loose, both from the expensive insurance he was required to help pay for (by dint of his dues) as a precondition of membership, and from any legal defense paid for by the organization. What will happen to Larry now?

Gentle reader, if you happen to have a son currently in a college fraternity, I would ask that you take several carbon dioxide–rich deep breaths from a paper bag before reading the next paragraph. I'll assume you are sitting down. Ready?

"I've recovered millions and millions of dollars from homeowners' policies," a top fraternal plaintiff's attorney told me. For that is how many of the claims against boys who violate the strict policies are paid: from their parents' homeowners' insurance. As for the exorbitant cost of providing the young man with a legal defense for the civil case (in which, of course, there are no public defenders), that is money he and his parents are going to have to scramble to come up with, perhaps transforming the family home into an ATM to do it. The financial consequences of fraternity membership can be devastating, and they devolve not on the 18-year-old "man" but on his planning-for-retirement parents.

LIKE THE SIX-BEER POLICY, the Fraternal Information and Programming Group's chillingly comprehensive crisis-management plan was included in its manual for many years. But in 2013, the plan suddenly disappeared from its pages. When asked why this was so, Dave Westol, a longtime FIPG board member, said, "Member organizations prefer to establish their own procedures, and therefore the section has been eliminated." However, many fraternities continue to rely on the group's advice for in-house risk management, and it is well worth examining if you want to know what takes place in the hours following many fraternity disasters. As it is described in the two most recent editions that I was able to obtain (2003 and 2007), the plan serves a dual purpose, at once benevolent and mercenary. The benevolent part is accomplished by the clear directive that injured parties are to receive immediate medical attention, and that all fraternity brothers who come into contact with the relevant emergency workers are to be completely forthright about what has taken place. And the rest? The plans I obtained recommend six important steps:

1. In the midst of the horror, the chapter president takes immediate, commanding, and inspiring control of the situation: "In times of stress, leaders step forward."

2. A call is made to the fraternity's crisis hotline or the national headquarters, no matter the hour: "Someone will be available. They would much rather hear about a situation from you at 3:27 a.m. than receive an 8:01 a.m. telephone call from a reporter asking for a comment about 'The situation involving your chapter at ___ ___.'"

3. The president closes the fraternity house to outsiders and summons all members back to the house: "Unorthodox situations call for unorthodox responses from leaders. Most situations occur at

night. Therefore, be prepared to call a meeting of all members and all pledged members as soon as possible, even if that is at 3 a.m."

4. One member—who has already received extensive media training—is put in charge of all relations with the press, an entity fraternities view as biased and often unscrupulous. The appointed member should be prepared to present a concise, factual, and minimally alarming account of what took place. For example: "A new member was injured at a social event."

5. In the case of the death of a guest or a member, fraternity brothers do not attempt direct contact with the deceased's parents. This hideous task is to be left to the impersonal forces of the relevant professionals. (I know of one family who did not know their son was in any kind of trouble until—many hours after his death, and probably long after his fraternity brothers had initiated the crisis-management protocol—their home phone rang and the caller ID came up with the area code of their boy's college and a single word: coroner.) If the dead person was a fraternity member who lived in the house, his brothers should return any borrowed items to his room and temporarily relocate his roommate, if he had one. Members may offer

to pack up his belongings, but "it is more likely the family will want to do this themselves." Several empty boxes might thoughtfully be left outside the room for this purpose.

6. Members sit tight until consultants from the national organization show up to take control of the situation and to walk them through the next steps, which often include the completion of questionnaires explaining exactly what happened and one-on-one interviews with the fraternity representatives. The anxious brothers are reminded to be completely honest and forthcoming in these accounts, and to tell the folks from national absolutely everything they know so that the situation can be resolved in the best possible manner.

As you should by now be able to see very clearly, the interests of the national organization and the individual members cleave sharply as this crisis-management plan is followed. Those questionnaires and honest accounts—submitted gratefully to the grown-ups who have arrived, the brothers believe, to help them—may return to haunt many of the brothers, providing possible cause for separating them from the fraternity, dropping them from the fraternity's insurance, laying the blame on them as individuals and not on the fraternity as the sponsoring organization. Indeed, the young men who typically rush so gratefully into the open arms of the representatives from their beloved national—an outfit to which they have pledged eternal allegiance—would be far better served by not talking to them at all, by walking away from the chapter house as quickly as possible and calling a lawyer.

So here is the essential question: In the matter of these disasters, are fraternities acting in an ethical manner, requiring good behavior from their members and punishing them soundly for bad or even horrific decisions? Or are they keeping a cool distance from the mayhem, knowing full well that misbehavior occurs with regularity ("most events take place at night") and doing nothing about it until the inevitable tragedy occurs, at which point they cajole members into incriminating themselves via a crisis-management plan presented as being in their favor?

The opposing positions on this matter are held most forcefully and expressed most articulately by two men: Douglas Fierberg, the best plaintiff's attorney in the country when it comes to fraternity-related litigation, and Peter Smithhisler, the CEO of the North American Interfraternity Conference, a trade organization representing 75 fraternities, among them all 32 members of the Fraternal Information and Programming Group. In a parallel universe, the two men would be not adversaries but powerful allies, for they have much in common: Both are robust Midwesterners in the flush of vital middle age and at the zenith of their professional powers; both possess more dark knowledge of college-student life and collegiate binge drinking than many, if not most, of the experts hired to study and quantify the phenomenon; both have built careers devoted to the lives and betterment of young people. But two roads diverged in the yellow wood, and here we are. One man is an avenger, a gun for hire, a person constitutionally ill-prepared to lose a fight; the other is a conciliator, a patient explainer, a man ever willing to lift the flap of his giant tent and welcome you inside. I have had long and wide-ranging conversations with both men, in which each put forth his perspective on the situation.

Fierberg is a man of obvious and deep intelligence, comfortable—in the way of alpha-male litigators—with sharply correcting a fuzzy thought; with using obscenities; with speaking derisively, even contemptuously, of opponents. He is also the man I would run to as though my hair were on fire if I ever found myself in a legal battle with a fraternity, and so should you. In a year of reporting this story, I have not spoken with anyone outside of the fraternity system who possesses a deeper understanding of its inner workings; its closely guarded procedures and money trails; and the legal theories it has developed over the past three decades to protect itself, often very successfully, from lawsuits. Fierberg speaks frequently and openly with the press, and because of this—and because of the reticence of senior members of the fraternity system to speak at length with meddlesome journalists—the media often reflect his attitude.

For all these reasons, Fierberg is generally loathed by people at the top of the fraternity world, who see him as a money-hungry lawyer who has chosen to chase their particular ambulance, and whose professed zeal for reforming the industry is a sham: What he wants is his share of huge damages, not systemic changes that would cut off the money flow. But in my experience of him, this is simply not the case. Sure, he has built a lucrative practice. But he is clearly passionate about his cause and the plight of the kids—some of them horribly injured, others dead—who comprise his caseload, along with their shattered parents.

"Until proven otherwise," Fierberg told me in April of fraternities, "they all are very risky organizations for young people to be involved in." He maintains that fraternities "are part of an industry that has tremendous risk and a tremendous history of rape, serious injury, and death, and the vast majority share common risk-management policies that are fundamentally flawed. Most of them are awash in alcohol. And most if not all of them are bereft of any meaningful adult supervision." As for the risk-management policies themselves: "They are primarily designed to take the nationals' fingerprints off the injury and deaths, and I don't believe that they offer any meaningful provisions." The fraternity system, he argues, is "the largest industry in this country directly involved in the provision of alcohol to underage people." The crisis-management plans reveal that in "the *foreseeable future*" there may be "the death or serious injury" of a healthy young person at a fraternity function.

And then there is Peter Smithhisler, who is the senior fraternity man *ne plus ultra*: unfailingly, sometimes elaborately courteous; careful in his choice of words; unflappable; and as unlikely to interrupt or drop the f-bomb on a respectful female journalist as he would be to join the Communist Party. He is the kind of man you would want on your side in a tough spot, the kind of man you would want mentoring your son through the challenging passage from late adolescence to young manhood. He believes that the fraternity experience at its best constitutes an appeal to a young man's better angels: Through service, leadership training, and accountability for mistakes, a brother can learn the valuable lessons he will need to become "a better dad, a better teacher, a better engineer, a better pilot, a better 'insert career here.'" Spend some time talking with Pete Smithhisler, and you can go from refusing to allow your son to join a fraternity to demanding he do so. Indeed, the day after I talked with him, I happened to be at a social gathering where I met two women whose sons had just graduated from college. "The fraternity was what saved him," one mother said with great feeling. Her son had waited until sophomore year to rush, and freshman year he had been so lonely and unsure of himself that she had become deeply worried about him. But everything changed after he pledged. He had friends; he was happy. When he'd had to have some surgery while at school, his brothers had visited him almost around the clock, bringing him food, keeping up his spirits, checking in with his doctors and charming his nurses. "If only I could have gotten my son to join one," the other mom said, wistfully. "I kept trying, but he wouldn't do it." Why had she wished he'd pledged a fraternity? "He would have been so much more connected to the college," she said. "He would have had so many other opportunities."

Smithhisler was honest about the fact that he is at the helm of an outfit that supports organizations in which young people can come to terrible fates. "I wrestle with it," he said, with evident feeling. His belief is that what's tarnishing the reputation of the fraternities is the bad behavior of a very few members, who ignore all the risk-management training that is requisite for membership, who flout policies that could not be any more clear, and who are shocked when the response from the home office is not to help them cover their asses but to ensure that— perhaps for the first time in their lives—they are held 100 percent accountable for their actions. And neither the fraternities nor the insurance company are hiding their warnings that a member could lose his coverage if he does anything outside of the policy. It's front and center in any discussion of a frat's alcohol policies; if you don't follow the policy or if you do anything illegal, you could lose your insurance.

One way you become a man, Smithhisler suggests, is by taking responsibility for your own mistakes, no matter how small or how large they might be. If a young man wants to join a fraternity to gain extensive drinking experience, he's making a very bad choice. "A policy is a policy is a policy," he said of the six-beer rule: Either follow it, get out of the fraternity, or prepare to face the consequences if you get caught. Unspoken but inherent in this larger philosophy is the idea that it is in a young man's nature to court danger and to behave in a foolhardy manner; the fraternity experience is intended to help tame the baser passions, to channel protean energies into productive endeavors such as service, sport, and career preparation.

In a sense, Fierberg, Smithhisler, and the powerful forces they each represent operate as a check and balance on the system. Personal-injury lawsuits bring the hated media attention and potential financial losses that motivate fraternities to improve. It would be a neat, almost a perfect, system, if the people wandering into it were not young, healthy college students with everything to lose.

If you want an object lesson in how all of this actually works—how fraternities exert their power over colleges, how college and university presidents can be reluctant to move unilaterally against dangerous fraternities, and how students can meet terrible fates as a result—there can be no better example than the $10 million Title IX lawsuit filed against Wesleyan University and the Beta Theta Pi fraternity. The plaintiff was a young woman who had been assaulted in the house, and who—in one of the bizarre twists so common to fraternity litigation—ended up being blamed by the university for her own assault.

WESLEYAN UNIVERSITY, in Middletown, Connecticut, is undergoing the kind of institutional transformation that our relentless fixation on *U.S. News & World Report* rankings has wrought for a number of colleges and universities in the past three decades. As great as its faculty may be— and it has included, over the years, some of the most renowned scholars in the world—it is the undergraduate population itself that constitutes its most impressive resource. Wesleyan is one of those places that has by now become so hard to get into that the mere fact of attendance is testament, in most cases, to a level of high-school preparation—combined with sheer academic ability— that exists among students at only a handful of top colleges in this country and that is almost without historical precedent. Wesleyan is a school with a large number of aspiring artists—many of whom took, and aced, AP Calculus as 11th-graders.

Still, what the university is perhaps most broadly famous for is its progressive politics, manifest in any number of actions, from the hiring of five Muslim chaplains in the

A

years since 9/11; to the use of the gender-neutral pronouns *ze* and *hir* in the campus newspaper; to the creation of a Diversity Education Facilitation Program. *The Princeton Review*, among other publications, has named Wesleyan America's most politically active campus, an encomium that appears on the university's website.

During Halloween weekend, Jane Doe got dressed up and went out with some of her friends. "I didn't have any alcohol to drink all night," she later told a police investigator.

Given these sensibilities, Wesleyan might not seem the type of institution likely to have a typical fraternity scene, but as we have observed, fraternities are older than political correctness. There are three all-male residential frats at Wesleyan, all founded in the 19th century and occupying a row of large houses on High Street; over the years, they have counted some of the university's most accomplished and loyal alumni among their members. If you raise the topic of fraternity alumni with a college president in a private moment, he or she will emit the weary sigh of the ancients. The group includes some of the most financially generous and institutionally helpful former students a school may have. But try to do some small thing to bring the contemporary fraternity scene in line with current campus priorities, and you will hear from them—loudly—before you even hit send on the email.

By 2005, Wesleyan had taken such an action: It had pressured all three fraternities to offer residence, although not membership, to female students, if they wanted to be part of university-approved Program Housing. Wesleyan has a rare requirement. All undergraduates, barring those few who receive special allowances, must live either in dorms or in Program Housing. Integrating affinity group housing had lately been on the mind of the administration; recent lack of student interest in living in the Malcolm X House, for example, had ultimately led to that residence becoming racially integrated, a charged and in many respects unpopular administration decision. But there was no shortage of fraternity brothers wishing to live in their houses—nor were the houses owned by the university or located on university property, as the Malcolm X House was. Predictably, and perhaps not irrationally, many in the Greek community viewed this new edict as antagonistic toward their way of life.

Two of the fraternities nonetheless agreed to the new directive, retaining access to the buffet of advantages offered to frats that maintain an official relationship with their host universities. Alone among the group, Beta Theta Pi hewed to the oldest of fraternity values: independence. It refused to admit women residents, and thus forfeited its official recognition by the university. Strangely, however, Beta was able to have its cake and eat it too: Its members continued to live and party in the house much as they

A

previously had, renting dorm rooms on campus but living at the fraternity, with the full knowledge of the university. This put Wesleyan in a difficult spot; the house remained a popular location for undergraduate revelry, yet the school's private security force, Public Safety (or PSafe), had lost its authority to monitor behavior there. Meanwhile, fraternity alumni registered their disapproval of the new housing policy in time-honored fashion: "I will reluctantly shift my Wesleyan contributions to the Beta house, to do my part to provide students with the opportunities I was afforded during my time at Wesleyan," wrote a Beta alum from the class of 1964 to the university's then-president, Douglas Bennet. (Due to the potential for the appearance of a conflict of interest, James Bennet, Douglas Bennet's son and the editor in chief of *The Atlantic*, was recused from involvement with this piece.)

What followed was a long, strained period in which Beta brothers—among them a large percentage of the school's lacrosse team—ran an increasingly wild house. In turn, the administration became increasingly concerned about what was happening there, and through back channels began pressuring the fraternity to rejoin Program Housing. But the brothers didn't budge, and reports of dangerous activity—including assaults, burglaries, extreme drinking, and at least two car accidents linked to the house—mounted. Wesleyan had a powerful weapon at its disposal: At any time, it could have ordered the brothers to live in the dorm rooms they had paid for, consistent with the university's housing policy. But for whatever reason, it was loath to do so.

Why wouldn't the university act unilaterally to solve this problem? The answer may involve the deep power that fraternities exert over their host universities and the complex mix of institutional priorities in which fraternities are important stakeholders. Chief among them, typically, is fundraising. Shortly after the university tightened the housing policy for its fraternities, a new president, Michael Roth, was inaugurated. He came to Wesleyan—his own alma mater, where he had served as the president of his fraternity, Alpha Delta Phi—with an audacious goal: doubling the university's endowment. A man of prodigious personal, intellectual, and administrative talents, with a powerful love of Wesleyan, he was uniquely suited to this grand vision. But no sooner had he taken office than the world economy crashed, dragging down the Wesleyan endowment with it. The endowment was slowly recouping its losses when the university's odd and secretive chief investment officer and vice president of investments was abruptly fired and then sued for allegedly profiting from his position—the kind of scandal that can make potential donors think twice before committing money to an institution. (He denied the charges; the case settled for an undisclosed amount in April 2012.) In this challenging fundraising environment, taking decisive and punitive action against a fraternity would almost certainly come at a financial cost.

In February of 2010, the university tried a new tack: Wesleyan suddenly dropped the requirement for fraternities to house women. And yet still Beta refused to rejoin the fold and enter Program Housing. By March, the university at last took a decisive action. It sent a strongly worded email to the entire Wesleyan community, including the parents of all undergraduates, warning students to stay away from the Beta house. The email described "reports of illegal and unsafe behavior on the premises," although it specified only one such behavior, a relatively minor one: the overconsumption of alcohol, leading to hospital visits. This one example hardly matched the tone and language of the rest of the email, which was alarming: "We advise all Wesleyan students to avoid the residence"; "our concern for the safety and well-being of Wesleyan students living at the residence or visiting the house has intensified"; "we remain deeply concerned about the safety of those students who choose to affiliate with the house or attend events there against our advice."

The university was entirely in the right to send this email; it was an accurate report of a dangerous location. But many parents of Beta brothers were incensed—they felt that their sons had been unfairly maligned to a wide group of people by their own university. Thirty-seven Beta parents signed a letter of protest and sent it to Michael

Roth. In it, the parents asked the university to "issue a clarification which retracts the unsupported statements." No such email was sent—nor, in my view, should it have been. But that angry letter, sent by those outraged parents, was surely noted in the offices of the administration. The Beta brothers, meanwhile, had announced a plan to hire an off-duty Middletown cop to oversee their events, while continuing to deny PSafe access to their house. Roth was unsatisfied, saying, "The notion that Public Safety would have to get permission to enter a place where Wesleyan students, as Wesleyan students, are congregating is unacceptable."

The school year rolled on. Final exams came, and graduation, and then the students dispersed to their homes and internships and first jobs. Summer ripened into fall, and Wesleyan's newest students bid goodbye to their high-school selves, packed up their bags and crates, and—with excitement and anxiety—traveled to Middletown. Surely these youngest, least experienced, and most vulnerable of Wesleyan's students would be sent the important email that the older ones and their parents had received about the dangerous and unaffiliated fraternity?

They were not. Yes, there undoubtedly would have been a cost to resending the email: more angry Beta parents, fraternity discontent, pressure from Beta alumni and the national organization. But just as clearly, great good could have come from sending it; student safety was at

A

risk. University trepidation and fraternity intransigence were about to produce a tort case. Its plaintiff: a young woman known to us as Jane Doe—18 years old, freshly arrived at Wesleyan from her home in Maryland, as eager as any other new student to experience the excitement of college life.

During Halloween weekend, Jane Doe got dressed up and went out with some of her friends to sample the student parties on and around campus. "I didn't have any alcohol to drink all night," she later told a police investigator in a sworn statement. "I usually don't drink, and I hang out with people who don't drink either." At the Beta house, she was "immediately spotted by this guy" who did not introduce himself but started dancing with her. "I was happy that someone was dancing with me," she told the policeman, "because I got all dressed up." The man she was dancing with would turn out not to be a Beta member or even a Wesleyan student at all. His name was John O'Neill, and he was the ne'er-do-well high-school-lacrosse teammate of one of the Beta brothers. O'Neill lived in his mother's basement and, according to a Yorktown, New York, police detective, had been arrested for selling pot out of an ice-cream truck earlier that year. That wild fraternity houses are often attractive party locations for unsavory characters is a grim reality. After O'Neill had danced with Jane Doe for about 30 minutes, half a dozen of his pals came over (dressed, as he was, in Halloween costumes consisting of old soccer uniforms) and asked him whether he wanted to smoke some pot upstairs. Jane agreed to go along, although she had no plans to smoke. The group arranged itself in a small bedroom, with Jane sitting next to O'Neill on a couch. He put his arm around her, which was fine with her, and she slipped off her shoes because her feet hurt.

The group then moved to a second room, where the men continued smoking. When the other men had finished smoking, they got up to leave, and Jane, too, stood up and began putting on her shoes, preparing to follow them out, but O'Neill closed the bedroom door and locked it. "What's up?" she asked. He began kissing her, which she at first submitted to, but then pulled away. "He probably thought that I wanted to hook up with him, but I didn't," she reported. She started for the door again, but he grabbed her by the shoulders and pushed her down onto the couch. "What are you doing?" she cried. "Stop it."

According to the victim's sworn statement, here's what happened next. O'Neill got on top of Jane, straddling her chest and shoulders so she couldn't move; pulled down his shorts; and shoved his penis into her mouth. She struggled, and bit his penis. He slapped her and called her a bitch. Then he pulled up her dress, yanked off her tights, and forced his penis into her vagina. "The more you try, the faster you are going to get out of here," he said, and

A

covered her mouth with his hand so she couldn't scream for help. Some 10 minutes later, it was over. Jane pulled on her tights and ran downstairs and out of the fraternity house. On the street, hysterical, she ran into a male friend and asked him to walk her back to her dorm. Inside, she found a girlfriend who comforted her, staying nearby while she showered, giving her cookies, reading to her until she fell asleep. Following some spectacular bungling on Wesleyan's part (for instance, no one was at Health Services to help her, because it was a weekend), Jane went to the health center on Monday, then to two deans, and eventually, after her parents and brother strongly encouraged her to do so, to the police. The criminal-justice system began its swift, efficient process, resulting in O'Neill's conviction. (He was initially charged with first-degree sexual assault and first-degree imprisonment, but eventually pleaded no contest to lesser charges of third-degree assault and first-degree imprisonment. He was sentenced to 15 months in prison.)

John O'Neill was not a member of Beta Theta Pi, but fraternities are no strangers to acts of violence committed in their houses by nonmembers. The fraternity followed the standard playbook, expressing sympathy for all victims of sexual assault and reasserting its zero-tolerance policy for such crimes. The brothers cooperated fully with the police and other authorities, which led to the capture of the criminal; and the actions of the individual assailant were forcefully asserted to have been in no way conducted under the auspices of the fraternity.

But back on campus, this level of coolheaded professionalism was nowhere to be seen. A second email regarding Beta was sent out, this one attesting to *reports* (plural) of sexual assaults at the fraternity house "during recent parties"; noting that these reports "renewed our concern" expressed in the email sent before Jane Doe's enrollment; and strongly encouraging students to stay away from the house. Next, Michael Roth issued an edict that he would come to regret: No Wesleyan student could so much as visit *any* private society lacking recognition by the university. His declaration was obviously intended to shut down Beta or bring it into the fold—but it did so in the same roundabout manner in which the university had been dealing with Beta all along. Its implications were unintentionally far-reaching, and Wesleyan students immediately protested it, holding "Free Beta" rallies; in one instance, a car full of young men shouted the slogan as Jane Doe walked miserably back to campus after visiting the police station. That student sympathies would array themselves so strongly on the side of a fraternity in whose chapter house a sexual assault had occurred, and so negligibly on the side of the young victim of that assault, was the kind of eccentric Wesleyan reaction that no one could have predicted.

Meanwhile, a nonprofit organization called FIRE, the Foundation for Individual Rights in Education, got involved, sending an open letter to President Roth informing him that his action posed a grave threat to Wesleyan students' right to the freedom of association, violated the university's own "Joint Statement on the Rights and Freedoms of Students," and might have consequences extending even to the local Elks Lodge and the Middletown Italian Society—hardly hives of Wesleyan undergraduate activity, but the organization had made its point.

The embattled president retrenched: He published a statement titled "Housing Policy and Threats to Student Freedom," in which he deemed his previous policy "just too broad," retracted most of it, and—in what has become a hallmark of his tenure—lavishly praised the student activism that it had engendered. "I want to thank the vocal Wesleyan undergraduates for reminding their president to be more careful in his use of language, and to be more attentive to student culture. Of course, I should have known this already, but hey, I try to keep learning."

Strictly speaking, the newest policy should not have ended the Free Beta protests, nor should it have assuaged activists' concern about threats to student freedom—because Roth also asserted in his statement that nothing had changed in regards to Beta: If the fraternity did not join Program Housing by the start of the next semester, the fraternity would be "off limits" to all students. Anyone who violated this rule would face "significant disciplinary action." It was high-handed treatment, it trampled on students' freedom of association, and it was entirely within Roth's rights. Wesleyan is a private university, and as such can establish requirements about students' private behavior essentially at the whim of the administration—the "Joint Statement on the Rights and Freedoms of Students" be damned. And it worked. The Free Beta protests ended, the fraternity agreed to rejoin Program Housing, student activism moved on to its next pressing target of opportunity, and the Beta brothers enjoyed a defrosting of their relationship with the university.

It turned out that in the heel of the hunt, with the situation at the Beta house becoming so out of control that the Middletown police department was aggressively investigating the alleged violent rape of a Wesleyan student, the university finally decided to act unilaterally against Beta, imposing a potentially unpopular decision that would surely go a long way toward improving student safety. Why hadn't it done so earlier? Why had it spent so many years in protracted, back-channel negotiations with the fraternity, in a pointless campaign to cajole it into voluntarily rejoining Program Housing, when it could have pulled the trigger on this effective solution at any time? And—most pressing of all—why had it taken the assault of a freshman to get the university to finally take decisive action?

All of these questions were perhaps most pressing to Jane Doe, who had not gone back home to Maryland to nurse her wounds in private. Justly outraged by what had happened to her, as well as by what she saw as her own university's complicity in it, she had joined forces with Douglas Fierberg, and together they built a case of formidable moral rightness.

Jane Doe filed a $10 million lawsuit in federal court against, in the main, Wesleyan and Beta Theta Pi, asserting that the events leading up to, including, and following Halloween weekend 2010 constituted a violation of the rights guaranteed her through Title IX legislation. It's hard to see how she wasn't right about this. She ended up withdrawing from a top university because that institution refused to take actions that could have prevented the assault, or, at the very least, to provide her with information she could have used to protect herself from it.

Wesleyan's affirmative defense—part of its answers to the lawsuit's complaint—was of a mien familiar to anyone with knowledge of how the civil litigation of rape cases unfolds. It was expedient, a shrewd legal strategy designed to protect the university from a guilty verdict and a huge settlement. It was also morally repugnant. Wesleyan's president has said the university is engaged in a "battle against sexual assault"; has averred—as recently as last

April—that "survivors of assault must be supported in every way possible"; and has committed himself to ending the "epidemic" of sexual violence at Wesleyan. But here's how the university supported this particular survivor of sexual violence, who dared to stand up against the mighty force of Wesleyan with her claim of mistreatment: It blamed her for getting raped.

According to Wesleyan—courageous combatant in the "battle against sexual assault"—Jane Doe was responsible for her own rape because she was "not alert to situations that could be misinterpreted"; "did not remain in a public place [but rather went to a private room] with a person with whom she was unfamiliar"; "failed to make reasonable and proper use of her faculties and senses"; and failed "to exercise reasonable care for her own safety." I disagree. Jane Doe's sworn statement describes a series of sound actions taken toward the care of her own safety—including making the decision not to drink or use drugs, attempting to exit a room when she was about to be left alone in it with an unfamiliar man who had used drugs, and attempting to fight him off when he began attacking her. But she was physically restrained by a powerfully built man intent on assaulting her.

SURELY THERE ARE MANY collegiate sexual encounters that fall into legally ambiguous territory; a number of Americans, among them reasonable people of good will,

A

believe that "regretted sex" on the part of jilted coeds is as responsible for college "rape culture" as is male aggression. This is not one of those cases. This was a violent assault that occasioned a police investigation, an arrest, criminal charges, a conviction, and a jail sentence. To suggest—let alone to assert in federal court—that this event was the result of Jane Doe's negligence would be ugly if it were part of a rape case involving, say, the US military. For it to be asserted on behalf of an American university against one of its own young students is even more astonishing. What it reveals is less Wesleyan's true attitude toward assault and its victims (surely there was distaste within the Wesleyan inner sanctum for the line of attack waged in the university's name against its former student) than the marshy ground of the progressive politics that underpins so much of the university's rhetoric. It's fine to announce a war against sexual violence—but, once the chips are down, it's quite another thing to write a $10 million check. Wesleyan's sexual-assault victims could be forgiven for assuming that, no matter what, their institution would never blame them for their attack. (Michael Roth and Wesleyan repeatedly declined to discuss the case, or anything related to this article, on the grounds that they did not want to comment on confidential matters pertaining to a lawsuit. Later, when *The Atlantic* sent President Roth an advance copy of the article a few days before publication, the university provided an official response. Douglas

Fierberg, Jane Doe's attorney, also declined to talk about her case or anything relating to it, citing similar reasons.)

This January, after publishing a withering series of reports on fraternity malfeasance, the editors of Bloomberg .com published an editorial with a surprising headline: "Abolish Fraternities." It compared colleges and universities to companies, and fraternities to units that "don't fit into their business model, fail to yield an adequate return or cause reputational harm." The comparison was inexact, because colleges aren't businesses, and fraternities do not operate as divisions of a corporate structure helmed by institutions of higher learning. They are private societies, old and powerful, as deeply woven into the history of American higher education as nonreligious study. A college or university can choose, as Wesleyan did, to end its formal relationship with a troublesome fraternity, but—if that fiasco proves anything—keeping a fraternity at arm's length can be more devastating to a university and its students than keeping it in the fold.

Clearly, the contemporary fraternity world is beset by a series of deep problems, which its leadership is scrambling to address, often with mixed results. No sooner has a new "Men of Principle" or "True Gentlemen" campaign been rolled out—with attendant workshops, measurable goals, initiatives, and mission statements—than reports of a lurid disaster in some prominent or far-flung chapter undermine the whole thing. Clearly, too, there is a Grand

A

Canyon–size chasm between the official risk-management policies of the fraternities and the way life is actually lived in countless dangerous chapters.

Articles like this one are a source of profound frustration to the fraternity industry, which believes itself deeply maligned by a malevolent press intent on describing the bad conduct of the few instead of the acceptable—sometimes exemplary—conduct of the many. But when healthy young college students are gravely injured or killed, it's newsworthy. When there is a common denominator among hundreds of such injuries and deaths, one that exists across all kinds of campuses, from private to public, prestigious to obscure, then it is more than newsworthy: It begins to approach a national scandal.

Universities often operate from a position of weakness when it comes to fraternities—for far too long, this is what happened with Wesleyan and Beta Theta Pi. The one force that may exert pressure on the fraternities to exact real change is the lawsuit. Plaintiffs have stories to tell that are so alarming, fraternities may, perhaps, be forced to do business differently because of them.

Perhaps.

Last spring, Wesleyan sent yet another email about Beta Theta Pi to the student body. It reported that in the early-morning hours of April 7, a Wesleyan student contacted PSafe to report that she had been attacked at the Beta house. Interviewed by Wesleyan campus police, she reported that while she was at the house, an unknown male had knocked her to the floor, kicked and hit her, and then attempted to sexually assault her. During the assault, the suspect was distracted by a loud noise, and the young woman escaped. She was later treated at the Middletown hospital for several minor injuries.

In August, quietly and while students were away, Wesleyan and Beta Theta Pi settled with Jane Doe, who now attends college in another state.

A

I'LL TELL YOU THE
SECRET OF CANCER

August 2021

ARE YOU SOMEONE WHO ENJOYS the unsolicited opinions of strangers and acquaintances? If so, I can't recommend cancer highly enough. You won't even have the first pathology report in your hands before the advice comes pouring in. Laugh and the world laughs with you; get cancer and the world can't shut its trap.

Stop eating sugar; keep up your weight with milkshakes. Listen to a recent story on NPR; do _not_ read a recent story in _Time_ magazine. Exercise—but not too vigorously; exercise—_hard_, like Lance Armstrong. Join a support group, make a collage, make a collage _in_ a support group, collage the shit out of your cancer. Do you live near a freeway or drink tap water or eat food microwaved on plastic plates? That's what caused it. Do you ever think about suing? Do you ever wonder whether, if you'd just let some time pass, the cancer would have gone away on its own?

Before I got cancer, I thought I understood how the world worked, or at least the parts that I needed to know about. But when I got cancer, my body broke down so catastrophically that I stopped trusting what I thought and believed. I felt that I had to listen when people told me what to do, because clearly I didn't know anything.

Much of the advice was bewildering, and all of it was anxiety-producing. In the end, because so many people contradicted one another, I was able to ignore most of them. But there was one warning I heard from a huge number of people, almost every day, and sometimes two or three times a day: I had to stay positive. People who beat cancer have a great *positive attitude*. It's what distinguishes the survivors from the dead.

There are books about how to develop the positive attitude that beats cancer, and meditation tapes to help you visualize your tumors melting away. Friends and acquaintances would send me these books and tapes—and they would send them to my husband, too. We were both anxious and willing to do anything in our control.

But after a terrible diagnosis, a failed surgery, a successful surgery, and the beginning of chemotherapy, I just wasn't feeling very . . . up. At the end of another terrible day, my husband would gently ask me to sit in the living room so that I could meditate and think positive thoughts. I was nauseated from the drugs, tired, and terrified that I would leave my little boys without a mother. All I wanted to do was take my Ativan and sleep. But I couldn't do that. If I didn't change my attitude, I was going to die.

PEOPLE GET DIAGNOSED WITH cancer in different ways. Some have a family history, and their doctors monitor them for years. Others have symptoms for so long that the eventual diagnosis is more of a terrible confirmation than a shock. And then there are people like me, people who are going about their busy lives when they push open the door of a familiar medical building for a routine appointment and step into an empty elevator shaft.

The afternoon in 2003 that I found out I had aggressive breast cancer, my boys were almost 5. The biggest thing on my mind was getting the mammogram over with early enough that I could pick up some groceries before the babysitter had to go home. I put on the short, pink paper gown and thought about dinner. And then everything started happening really fast. Suddenly there was the need for a second set of films, then a sonogram, then the sharp pinch of a needle. In my last fully conscious moment as the person I once was, I remember asking the doctor if I should have a biopsy. The reason I asked was so that he could look away from the screen, realize that he'd scared me, and reassure me. "No, no," he would say; "it's completely benign." But he didn't say that. He said, "That's what we're doing right now."

Later I would wonder why the doctor hadn't asked my permission for the needle biopsy. The answer was that I had already passed through the border station that separates the healthy from the ill. The medical community and I were on new terms.

The doctor could see that I was in shock, and he seemed pretty rattled himself. He kept saying that he should call my husband. "You need to prepare yourself," he said, twice. And once: "It's aggressive." But I didn't want him to call my husband. I wanted to tear off my paper gown and never see that doctor, his office, or even the street where the building was located ever again. I had a mute, animal need to get the hell out of there. The news was so bad, and it kept getting worse. I couldn't think straight. My little boys were so small. They were my life, and they needed me.

Three weeks later, I was in the infusion center. Ask Google "What is the worst chemotherapy drug?" and the answer is Doxorubicin. That's what I got, as well as some other noxious pharmaceuticals. That oncologist filled me and my fellow patients up with so much poison that the sign on the bathrooms said we had to flush twice to make sure every trace was gone before a healthy person—a nurse, or a family member—could use the toilet. I was not allowed to hug my children for the first 24 hours after treatment, and in the midst of this absolute hell—in the midst of the poison and the crying and the sorrow and the terror—I was supposed to get a really great positive attitude.

A

The book we were given several copies of, which was first published in 1986 and has been reissued several times since, is titled *Love, Medicine and Miracles* and was written by a pediatric surgeon named Bernie Siegel. He seems less interested in exceptional scientific advances than in "exceptional patients." To be exceptional, you have to tell your body that you want to live; you have to say "No way" to any doctor who says you have a fatal illness. You have to become a channel of perfect self-love, and remember that "the simple truth is, happy people generally don't get sick." Old angers or disappointments can congeal into cancer. You need to get rid of those emotions, or they will kill you.

In 1989 a Stanford psychiatrist named David Spiegel published a study of women with metastatic breast cancer. He created a support group for half the women, whom he taught self-hypnosis. The other women got no extra social support. The results were remarkable: Spiegel reported that the women in the group survived twice as long as the other women. This study was hugely influential in modern beliefs about meditation and cancer survival. It showed up in the books my husband read to me, which were filled with other stories of miraculous healings, of patients defying the odds through their own emotional work. But I was so far behind. From the beginning I couldn't stop crying. I began to think I was hopeless and would never survive.

I needed help, and I remembered a woman my husband and I had talked to in the first week after my diagnosis. Both of us had found in those conversations our only experience of calm, our only reassurance that we were doing the right things. Anne Coscarelli is a clinical psychologist and the founder of the Simms/Mann-UCLA Center for Integrative Oncology, which helps patients and their families cope with the trauma of cancer. We had reached out to her when we were trying to understand my diagnosis. Now I needed her for much more.

For the first half hour in her office, we just talked about how sick I felt and how frightened I was. Then—nervously—I confessed: I wasn't doing the work of healing myself. I wasn't being positive.

"Why do you need to be positive?" she asked in a neutral voice.

I thought it should be obvious, but I explained: Because I didn't want to die!

Coscarelli remained just as neutral and said, "There isn't a single bit of evidence that having a positive attitude helps heal cancer."

What? That couldn't possibly be right. How did she know that?

"They study it all the time," she said. "It's not true."

David Spiegel was never able to replicate his findings about metastatic breast cancer. The American Cancer Society and the National Center for Complementary and

Integrative Health say there's no evidence that meditation or support groups increase survival rates. They can do all sorts of wonderful things, like reducing stress and allowing you to live in the moment instead of worrying about the next scan. I've learned, whenever I start to get scared, to do some yoga-type breathing with my eyes closed until I get bored. If I'm bored, I'm not scared, so then I open my eyes again. But I'm not alive today because of deep breathing.

When I began to understand that attitude doesn't have anything to do with survival, I felt myself coming up out of deep water. I didn't cause my cancer by having a bad attitude, and I wasn't going to cure it by having a good one.

And then Coscarelli told me the whole truth about cancer. If you're ready, I will tell it to you.

Cancer occurs when a group of cells divide in rapid and abnormal ways. Treatments are successful if they interfere with that process.

Everyone with cancer has a different experience, and different beliefs about what will help. I feel strongly that these beliefs should be respected—including the feelings of those who decide not to have any treatment at all. It's sadism to learn that someone is dangerously ill and to impose upon her your own set of unproven assumptions, especially ones that blame the patient for getting sick in the first place.

That meeting with Anne Coscarelli took place 18 years ago, and never once since then have I worried that my attitude was going to kill me. I've had several recurrences, all of them significant, but I'm still here, typing and drinking a Coke and not feeling super upbeat.

Before I left that meeting, I asked her one last question: Maybe I couldn't think my way out of cancer, but wasn't it still important to be as good a person as I could be? Wouldn't that karma improve my odds a little bit?

Coscarelli told me that, over the years, many wonderful and generous women had come to her clinic, and some of them had died very quickly. Yikes. I had to come clean: Not only was I un-wonderful. I was also kind of a bitch.

God love her, she came through with exactly what I needed to hear: "I've seen some of the biggest bitches come in, and they're still alive."

And that, my friends, was when I had my very first positive thought. I imagined all those bitches getting healthy, and I said to myself, *I think I'm going to beat this thing.*

A